# Assignments in
# Leisure and Tourism
## for GNVQ  Book I

**John Ward**

The Travel and Tourism Programme

**Stanley Thornes (Publishers) Ltd**

Published in 1993 by:
Stanley Thornes (Publishers) Ltd
Ellenborough House
Wellington Street
CHELTENHAM GL50 1YD
England

Reprinted 1993
Reprinted 1994

A catalogue record for this book is available from The British Library.

ISBN 0 7487 1668 8

Typeset by Stanley Thornes (Publishers) Ltd
Printed and bound in Great Britain by Hillman Printers Ltd., Frome

# Contents

## Unit 4: Marketing in leisure and tourism

# Introduction

## General

This book of assignments has been prepared primarily with the new General National Vocational Qualification (GNVQ) in mind, though many of the assignments should prove equally useful to students of other leisure and tourism courses.

One of the main purposes of GNVQs is to provide a national scheme of vocational qualifications which can stand alongside traditional academic qualifications and offer an attractive but rigorous alternative. They are intended to offer a broad-based approach, avoiding a concentration on very narrow vocational skills, which will better equip students either for entry into employment or progression into higher education. Consequently, assignments set on such courses need to be both enjoyable and demanding.

GNVQs are assessed largely on the basis of evidence collected during the course. These assignments are intended to generate a range of outcomes in a variety of forms. Some require student participation in discussion, role play and oral presentation; others demand a variety of written outcomes, including reports, letters, memoranda, diagrams and computer-generated information.

Many of the assignments are structured so that there are some tasks which can be done immediately, these being entirely based on the stimulus material which precedes them. Subsequent tasks will often require discussion and research and are likely to involve co-operative work. The tasks have been designed to generate the kind of evidence required for the cumulative assessment which is central to GNVQ courses

### Level of difficulty

GNVQs are aimed primarily at the 16–19 age group, but the long-term aim is to make them more widely available. Most students are likely to be on full-time school or college courses, in some cases combining GNVQs with GCSE and A or AS level courses.

GNVQs are being developed at four levels of difficulty, with Intermediate and Advanced levels likely to be in most demand in schools and colleges. Achieving a GNVQ at Intermediate level is intended to be the equivalent of taking four GCSE subjects; at Advanced it is intended to represent similar demands to those made on a student taking two A levels, if they complete 12 units, or three A levels if they complete 18. In other words the programmes are intended to appeal to the full ability range and not just to those considered unsuitable for academic courses. The assignments in this book reflect that aim by focusing on complex issues and providing opportunities for the development of a wide range of skills.

The structure of this book is based on the mandatory units required for GNVQ Advanced. Given the considerable overlap in the units at Intermediate and Advanced, however, many of the assignments should prove equally suitable for use at Intermediate.

### The leisure and tourism industry

Leisure and tourism is made up of a wide range of very different, but interdependent, activities and operations. These include accommodation, catering, transport, tourist attractions, sport, entertainment, the arts and other recreation and leisure activities. Its economic importance is proved by the fact that in 1991 tourist expenditure in Britain was around £25 billion. Around 7 per cent of employment in Britain is directly related to tourism.

Though leisure and tourism are growing industries in Britain, they are also changing. For example, traditional longer-stay holidays in British destinations are gradually being replaced by more short breaks, second holidays and day trips. Demand for a range of leisure activities has risen, coinciding with the growing awareness of healthier lifestyles. Forecasts suggest that this growth will continue, but will face strong competition from overseas and especially within the single European market.

The implications of this for future planning suggest that improving quality and value for money is of prime importance and that this can only be achieved by increasing standards of training and professionalism. Vocational qualifications have a part to play in creating a more skilled and knowledgeable work force. Schemes such as the Travel and Tourism Programme, supported by American Express, Forte Hotels, The British Tourist Authority/English Tourist Board, along with Thomas Cook, have shown the industry's commitment to improving knowledge, understanding and skills.

### The importance of industry links

Though it is not a requirement that teachers of leisure and tourism GNVQ must have worked at some time in a related occupational area, it is essential that local industry links are established. Students are not required to complete a period of work experience either, but their understanding of the issues facing employees in leisure and tourism are likely to be limited if such links are not established. Students have to know what determines business success, what factors it has to cope with which are outside its control and they have to learn how to develop realistic and viable solutions to practical business problems. The advice and experience of outsiders increases the likelihood that what students are learning reflects practice in the industry itself.

## Tutor Guide to the Units in Books 1 and 2

### Book 1

### Unit 1: Investigating the leisure and tourism industry

By comparison with the other seven units, Unit 1 covers potentially a vast amount of ground. Its scope makes it important to be selective in providing or suggesting resources. It would be easy to present students with an overwhelming amount of historical and statistical data which might prove discouraging.

Although there is no requirement to approach the units in a specific order, Unit 1 does contain some fundamental issues, an understanding of which is important at the outset. In particular it deals with definitions of leisure and tourism, as well as with their social, economic, cultural and environmental impacts.

Students may encounter some difficulty in obtaining detailed information about the funding of some leisure and tourism facilities. It is worth checking in advance to find out the extent of the confidentiality of such information.

## Unit 2: Maintaining health, safety and security

The intention is that this unit should focus on a specific facility. The assignments cover a number of facilities, however, so that a wider range of issues can be represented. The emphasis on regulation and legislation creates the potential for much very dry reading material. The essential points and applications of relevant legislation to specific work places will be more easily assimilated than the full text of Acts of Parliament or Health and Safety Codes of Practice.

Nevertheless reference to codes of practice and safety standards is necessary and there will be a cost if these are bought from organisations like the Health and Safety Executive or the British Standards Institution.

## Unit 3: Providing customer care

Customer care is vital to most parts of the leisure and tourism industry. Many larger organisations use commercially produced training material, such as Video Arts, but others run their own training programmes, and ideas from some of these are incorporated into the assignments.

Though its importance is undeniable, many of the essential principles of customer care are not particularly complex and are common to sectors outside leisure and tourism. The skills involved are often described in very general terms – communication, rapport or efficiency – and these have to be broken down into stages and specific examples. Role plays are particularly useful in showing the relevance of individual skills to particular leisure and tourism contexts.

## Unit 4: Marketing in leisure and tourism

This unit focuses on the whole marketing process, from identifying customer needs through to planning promotional campaigns.

In most leisure and tourism businesses marketing is firmly controlled by a budget which may well be based on estimates of future performance. Nor is the process of marketing evaluation always a very exact science. Apart from obvious leaps in sales figures, evaluation may take the form of personal impressions and reports.

**Book 2**

## Unit 5: Planning for an event or function

The events or functions featured in these assignments include both the real and the simulated. The latter sometimes has the advantage of introducing a wider range of issues and constraints into the planning process.

As a planning exercise, this unit encourages group work and problem-solving and should offer the opportunity to develop core skills. The assignments cover extremes of scale, from the national to the local, in order to emphasise both broad planning issues and more specific practical details.

## Unit 6: Maintaining information services

Many students will already be familiar with techniques of information handling, especially those using computer technology.

The assignments included reflect both the need for good information services and approaches taken to achieving them in different leisure and tourism contexts.

Dealing with issues of confidentiality and security may prove difficult for some students. For obvious reasons some leisure and tourism businesses are reluctant to release sensitive information, for example about financial performance or personnel. They may permit a teacher or lecturer to 'fictionalise' some data and then allow its use.

## Unit 7: Working in teams

The assignments in this unit explore the key principles of team working, as well as looking at some specific examples.

Students should find that research into working practices which they have to do for Units 2, 4 and 8 for example, will enable them to explore how these principles are put into practice in other contexts.

## Unit 8: Evaluating the performance of facilities

The depth of evaluation studies carried out in leisure and tourism is often a matter of resources. Where detailed research has been undertaken, professional agencies are often involved.

The assignments reflect the variety of approaches by featuring a very small operation (a guest house) as well as examining aspects of much larger ones like airports or major visitor attractions.

## Combination of units and elements

Each of the 8 units is divided into elements, but student activities may cover more than one element at a time. It is equally possible to plan assignments which cover requirements in more than one unit. Research conducted at a single tourist attraction could provide a range of outcomes. For example, Assignments 4.8, 7.1 and 8.1 are all based on Beaulieu. Studying a theme, such as the environmental impact of leisure and tourism, would enable students to establish links between Assignments 1.7, 2.5, 4.5, 5.6 and 8.4. A local study of leisure provision could lead to various combinations of Assignments 1.4, 2.1, 3.3, 4.4 and 6.3.

## Core skills

Three core skills are incorporated into GNVQs: Communication, Application of Number and Information Technology. Like most skills, these are best developed in a realistic context; and they are not therefore isolated in this book but are incorporated within the context of a range of assignments.

Because of the nature of their content, some units lend themselves particularly to developing individual core skills. Thus Communication is a vital element in Units 3 and 7, since neither Customer Care nor Working in Teams could exist without it! Similarly Unit 6, Maintaining Information Services, is more dependent on Information Technology skills than some others.

The following examples highlight assignments which could be especially useful in developing core skills:

## Communication

Inevitably very few of the assignments do not require the exercise of Communication skills at some point. The following list illustrates the varied approach to developing these:
1.4, 1.7, 1.9, 2.3, 2.5, 2.6, 2.9, 3.2, 3.3, 3.5, 3.7, 4.3, 4.9, 5.1 5.5, 5.9, 6.4, 6.6, 7.1, 7.4, 7.5, 8.4, 8.5, 8.6.

## Application of Number

1.1, 2.4, 2.5, 3.1, 3.9, 4.1, 4.2, 4.4, 4.7, 4.9, 5.3, 5.6, 6.7, 7.2, 8.1, 8.2, 8.5, 8.6.

## Information Technology

1.11, 6.1, 6.2, 6.3, 6.4, 6.5, 6.8.

In addition Information Technology skills could be applied in the design and presentation of many of the written assignments.

## Active learning

These assignments are intended to encourage students to work both on their own and in small groups. Though resource material is provided, it generally also acts as a starting point for further research. The assignments encourage students to develop planning skills, judgement and initiative. Frequent choices are offered and students may wish to add further appropriate options of their own.

## The range of activities

These assignments encourage the production of evidence from students in a variety of forms and from a variety of sources. GNVQs encourage the use of investigations, surveys, case studies and planning and designing activities. This book contains many such practical tasks, providing in many cases source material on which they can be wholly or partly based.

Planning and design tasks include the consideration of posters, notices, floor plans, itineraries, business plans, contingency plans and development proposals. The assignments can be used to generate among other things reports, analyses, speeches or presentations, codes of practice and guidance notes. Responses will be written and oral. Students are challenged to identify a range of principles, qualities, changes, arguments and issues relevant to leisure and tourism. The tasks frequently encourage discussion, in small groups and in role, in order to arrive at consensus or to identify a range of conclusions.

## Progression

Since research degrees are now awarded for a whole range of leisure and tourism studies, GNVQs provide a number of opportunities for progression. Apart from moving, for example, from Level 2 to Level 3, successful students can move into higher education to follow diploma or degree courses. In some cases it may be possible to combine these with employment, so that the qualification forms part of the individual's overall training.

## Glossary

Certain words and phrases specific to the leisure and tourism industry have been highlighted in the text. An explanation of these terms will be found in the glossary on page 91.

*Assignments in Leisure and Tourism*

## GNVQ2 Leisure and Tourism: Summary of mandatory units

### Unit 1  Investigating leisure and tourism Level 2

**1.1** Investigate the leisure and tourism industry in a locality
**1.2** Investigate leisure and tourism services and products provided by a facility
**1.3** Identify employment opportunities in leisure and tourism

### Unit 3  Customer service Level 2

**3.1** Investigate the customer care strategies of facilities
**3.2** Provide assistance to customers
**3.3** Maintain records

### Unit 2  Contributing to an event/service Level 2

**2.1** Contribute to planning an event/service with others
**2.2** Prepare schedules for an event/service with others
**2.3** Plan own contribution to a given event/service
**2.4** Undertake a role in an event/service with others
**2.5** Contribute to the evaluation of an event/service

### Unit 4  Promoting products and services Level 2

**4.1** Investigate the function of promotion in leisure and tourism
**4.2** Evaluate the success of a promotional campaign
**4.3** Report on the design of a promotional campaign
**4.4** Prepare an outline promotional campaign

## GNVQ3 Leisure and Tourism: Summary of mandatory units

### Unit 1  Investigating the leisure and tourism industry Level 3

**1.1** Describe the scale and contexts of the leisure and tourism industry
**1.2** Investigate UK leisure and tourism products
**1.3** Investigate the variety of local services and products
**1.4** Identify sources of income for leisure and tourism facilities

### Unit 5  Planning for an event Level 3

**5.1** Propose options for an event
**5.2** Present a plan for an event
**5.3** Allocate roles and personnel in an event

### Unit 2  Maintaining health, safety and security Level 3

**2.1** Report on the health, safety, and security arrangements in a facility
**2.2** Propose ways of enhancing the health and safety of customers and staff
**2.3** Propose ways of enhancing security in leisure and tourism

### Unit 6  Providing management information services Level 3

**6.1** Plan a management information service
**6.2** Select and provide management information
**6.3** Record and process management information

### Unit 3  Providing customer service Level 3

**3.1** Identify the function of customer service in leisure and tourism facilities
**3.2** Plan a customer care programme
**3.3** Provide customer service
**3.4** Evaluate the operation of the customer care programme

### Unit 7  Working in teams Level 3

**7.1** Investigate how leisure and tourism work teams operate
**7.2** Work with others in teams
**7.3** Evaluate team performance

### Unit 4  Marketing in leisure and tourism Level 3

**4.1** Identify market needs for products and services
**4.2** Identify market opportunities
**4.3** Plan promotional activities
**4.4** Evaluate promotional activities

### Unit 8  Evaluating the performance of facilities Level 3

**8.1** Research the organisational objectives of facilities
**8.2** Plan the evaluation of a facility's performance
**8.3** Evaluate the performance of a facility

Mandatory units for General National Vocational Qualifications offered by Business and Technology Education Council, City and Guilds and RSA Examinations Board from September 1993

# Acknowledgements

The author and publishers would like to thank the following organisations for permission to reproduce photographs and other material:

Bath Tourism Marketing (page 2); Olympian Health Club, St James Court Hotel (page 8); Cumbria Tourist Board (page12); Architext Publications (page 16); The English Tourist Board (page 17); Zac Macaulay, photographer, Walton-on-Thames (page 24); Stuart Baynes Photography, Bath (page 26); Bales Tours Ltd (pages 54–5); CNN Marketing Ltd (pages 71–2); A Day at the Wells (page 74); Paul Cordwell (page 77, top left); Phil Hill (page 77, top right); Tony Stone Images and The Telegraph Colour Library for the cover photographs. All other photographs were supplied by the author.

Every effort has been made to contact copyright holders and we apologise if any have been overlooked.

**The Travel and Tourism Programme**

An interesting feature of leisure and tourism is its increasing recognition of the importance of education as a means of encouraging young people, teachers and parents to give consideration to what is rapidly becoming the world's largest industrial sector.

Students are being encouraged to view the industries both from the standpoint of discriminating consumers and as career options. With the aim of fostering this dual perspective, the Travel and Tourism Programme, supported by American Express, Forte Hotels, and the British Tourist Authority/English Tourist Board, along with Thomas Cook, has willingly enabled these materials to be written.

John Ward is Professional Officer with the Travel and Tourism Programme.

# Unit 1 Investigating the leisure and tourism industry

## 1.1 What is leisure and tourism?

**Develops knowledge and understanding of the following element:**
1    Describe the scale and contexts of the leisure and tourism industry

**Supports development of the following core skills:**
Application of number level 3: Gather and process data (Task 1)
Communication level 3: Use images to illustrate points made in writing and discussion;
      Application of number level 3: Interpret and present mathematical data (Task 2)

A prominent representative of the industry, asked to explain the scope of the leisure and tourism industry, might reply along the following lines:

*Tourism is about providing facilities and services that visitors need. This includes all their travel arrangements, their accommodation, what they need to eat and drink, the activities they want to do and the services they need to use during the visit. So it is not surprising to find that leisure and tourism is a complex industry which includes everything from large organisations like international hotel chains and international airlines right down to small operations like souvenir kiosks and independent guides.*

*It is further complicated by the fact that many parts of the leisure and tourism industry are used by the local community as well as by visitors. Restaurants, public transport, museums and leisure centres provide services which have to meet the needs of both visitors and local residents, whether or not these needs conflict.*

*Tourism services are provided by both the **public** and **private sectors**, as well as by voluntary organisations. Accommodation is generally owned by private companies, as are many transport services. British Rail is still within the public sector, although there are of course plans to **privatise** it in the near future. Tour operators and travel agents are mainly to be found in the private sector. Perhaps the biggest mixture of ownership is in the area of attractions which may be run by local authorities, public bodies, charitable organisations or commercial companies.*

*There is an increasing trend for the larger companies involved in leisure and tourism to widen their interests. They may seek to become more international by purchasing interests in overseas companies, as in the case of British Airways' recent interest in other European and American airlines; or they may buy an interest in a leisure and tourism company as a **subsidiary** to their main interest. The well-known brewing company Bass, for example, is also the owner of the Holiday Inn International hotel group. Some companies seek to expand by purchasing an interest in operations which are similar to their own. The Tussauds Group, for example, in addition to the famous waxworks in London, also owns Alton Towers, Chessington World of Adventures, Rock Circus and Warwick Castle.*

*The leisure and tourism industry in the United Kingdom is more widespread than most of our traditional industries. It is coastal, rural and urban. It includes everything from the countryside pursuits associated with farm-based accommodation to the scientific and industrial centres and museums found in places like Stoke-*

on-Trent, Ironbridge and Manchester. Our national heritage, in particular our regional history, customs, crafts and architecture, is still able to draw visitors both to traditional historic towns like York and Bath, and also to new attractions like The White Cliffs Experience or The Tales of Robin Hood.

I would like to conclude by dispelling a common myth, that the leisure and tourism industry's activities are confined to the summer months. The business traveller, for example, needs services all the year round. Modern working conditions mean that many people have leisure time both at weekends and during the week throughout the whole year. People have always taken day excursions in the autumn and spring, but there has been a major growth in the last few years in the number of people taking short break holidays. A large number of these are associated with special interests, many of which are indoor activities, and there is a growing provision of indoor and all-weather leisure facilities. This means that there are more people who consider taking a break outside the traditional summer season.'

*Roman Baths Museum Bath: our national heritage is still able to draw visitors to traditional historic sites.*

## Your tasks

1 The above speech is to be made at a conference, but the planners decide that it does not contain sufficient data to support the main points they wish to make.
   Use your own research to produce some figures, statistics and additional examples which could strengthen the impact of the speech.

2 Design and produce a series of four overhead projections (OHPs) which could be used to illustrate the speech effectively.

# 1.2 Interpreting statistics

**Develops knowledge and understanding of the following element:**
1    Describe the scale and contexts of the leisure and tourism industry
**Supports development of the following core skills:**
Application of number level 3: Interpret and present mathematical data (Task 1)
Communication level 3: Take part in discussions (Task 2)

Statistics are information in the form of numbers, usually set out in columns or tables. The numbers given are often based on estimates. For example, a sample of a thousand people may be asked how they will vote at the next General Election: the answers they give will be used to estimate which party will get the most votes over the country as a whole. Since statistics record only numerical changes, and not the reasons for these changes, there is often disagreement about what the figures are actually telling us.

Look carefully at the three tables of tourism statistics which follow:

### Table 1 Employment in tourism-related industries June 1986 to June 1991

| Employees in employment (SIC Group) | June 1986 ('000) | June 1987 ('000) | June 1988 ('000) | June 1989 ('000) | June 1990 ('000) | June 1991 ('000) | % change June 1986/ June 1991 |
|---|---|---|---|---|---|---|---|
| Hotel and other tourist accommodation | 270.5 | 265.4 | 281.2 | 301.0 | 317.6 | 297.9 | +10 |
| Restaurants, cafés, etc. | 229.2 | 240.4 | 265.1 | 290.1 | 306.0 | 293.8 | +28 |
| Public houses and bars | 259.8 | 263.1 | 289.3 | 326.2 | 338.8 | 325.2 | +25 |
| Night clubs and licensed clubs | 138.2 | 136.9 | 140.5 | 140.4 | 142.3 | 144.9 | + 5 |
| Libraries, museums, art galleries, sports and other recreational services | 370.9 | 375.1 | 373.5 | 373.3 | 378.4 | 379.4 | + 2 |
| Total | 1268.6 | 1280.9 | 1349.7 | 1 431.0 | 1492.1 | 1441.3 | +14 |

*Source:* Employment Department

*Note:* Figures exclude Northern Ireland.
Figures are rounded, so that component figures may not add up to totals.

### Table 2 Employment in tourism-related industries (by sex) June 1990 and June 1991

| | Persons in employment ('000) | | |
|---|---|---|---|
| | Male | Female | Total |
| **June 1990** | | | |
| Hotel and other tourist accommodation | 123.8 | 193.8 | 317.6 |
| Restaurants, cafés, etc. | 124.2 | 181.8 | 306.0 |
| Public houses and bars | 104.1 | 234.7 | 338.8 |
| Night clubs and licensed clubs | 55.2 | 87.1 | 387.4 |
| Libraries, museums, art galleries, sports and other recreational services | 187.2 | 200.1 | 387.4 |
| Total | 594.5 | 897.6 | 1 492.1 |

*Source:* Employment Department

*Note:* Figures exclude Northern Ireland.
Figures are rounded, so that component figures may not add up to totals.

*Continued overleaf*

*Table 2 Continued*

| | Persons in employment ('000) | | |
|---|---|---|---|
| | Male | Female | Total |
| **June 1991** | | | |
| Hotel and other tourist accommodation | 116.1 | 181.9 | 297.9 |
| Restaurants, cafés, etc. | 123.6 | 170.2 | 293.8 |
| Public houses and bars | 99.6 | 225.6 | 325.2 |
| Night clubs and licensed clubs | 55.1 | 89.8 | 144.9 |
| Libraries, museums, art galleries, sports and other recreational services | 183.0 | 196.4 | 379.4 |
| Total | 577.5 | 863.9 | 1 441.3 |

*Source:* Employment Department

*Note:* Figures exclude Northern Ireland.
Figures are rounded, so that component figures may not add up to totals.

## Table 3  Employment in hotels by region June 1989

| | June 1989 Persons in employment | | % change June 1979/ June 1989 | % change June 1988/ June 1989 |
|---|---|---|---|---|
| | ('000) | % | | |
| South East | 367 | 33 | +33 | +2 |
| East Anglia | 34 | 3 | +34 | -1 |
| South West | 119 | 11 | +16 | +6 |
| West Midlands | 86 | 8 | +10 | +5 |
| East Midlands | 69 | 6 | +49 | +5 |
| Yorkshire and Humberside | 98 | 9 | +20 | +5 |
| North West | 108 | 10 | +8 | +4 |
| North | 63 | 6 | +4 | +7 |
| Wales | 52 | 5 | +10 | < 0.5% |
| Scotland | 110 | 10 | -3 | +4 |
| Great Britain | 1105 | 100 | +19 | +4 |

*Source:* Employment Department

*Note:* Figures exclude Northern Ireland. Regional estimates are subject to considerable sampling errors.

Figures include non-tourism related canteens and messes. Figures are rounded so that component figures may not add up to total 100%.

### Your tasks

1  Find evidence from the three tables to support or oppose the following claims:
   **a)** No tourism-related industry reported an increase in the numbers it employed between June 1990 and June 1991.

**b)** Since 1986 the accommodation sector has consistently employed more people than any other tourism-related industry.

**c)** Employment in hotel and catering in the South West is fairly typical of the pattern seen in the United Kingdom as a whole.

**d)** The percentage of women employed in tourism-related industries in June 1991 was greater than it had been twelve months earlier.

**e)** Employment figures in tourism-related industries show that people's leisure needs tend to remain much the same from one year to the next.

**f)** Employment patterns in hotel and catering show a marked difference between the North and the South of England.

**2** Prepare and deliver a short talk, explaining why tourism has offered, and will continue to offer, significant numbers of career opportunities to young people. You should draw on statistics given in Table 4, as well as on those in the Tables 1, 2 and 3, to support your evidence.

**Table 4 Value of tourism compared with other leading exports 1971 to 1990**

| Item | 1971 £m. | 1975 £m. | 1979 £m. | 1983 £m. | 1987 £m. | 1988 £m. | 1989 £m. | 1990 £m. | % change 1971/1990 |
|---|---|---|---|---|---|---|---|---|---|
| Non electrical machinery | 2087 | 3534 | 7610 | 9607 | 14 814 | 16 831 | 19 414 | 21 253 | +918 |
| Chemicals | 873 | 2145 | 4911 | 6933 | 10 519 | 11 331 | 12 350 | 13 183 | +1 410 |
| Transport equipment | 1308 | 2516 | 4434 | 5434 | 8636 | 9168 | 11 003 | 12 563 | +860 |
| Electrical machinery | 537 | 1248 | 2192 | 3284 | 5353 | 6102 | 7273 | 8336 | +1 452 |
| Petroleum products | 216 | 734 | 4158 | 12 501 | 8466 | 5576 | 5512 | 7478 | +3 362 |
| Sea transport* | 1595 | 2614 | 3717 | 2923 | 3122 | 3358 | 3710 | 3653 | +129 |
| Non-metallic mineral manufactures | 391 | 720 | 1714 | 1996 | 2654 | 2974 | 3199 | 3191 | +716 |
| Iron and steel | 403 | 682 | 1278 | 1331 | 2186 | 2392 | 2894 | 3036 | +653 |
| Textiles | 444 | 729 | 1339 | 1285 | 1886 | 1935 | 2205 | 2447 | +451 |
| Civil aviation* | 225 | 423 | 1100 | 1765 | 1840 | 1859 | 2168 | 2525 | +1 022 |
| **Tourism*** | 649 | 1625† | 3542† | 5023† | 7738† | 7685† | 8695† | 9812† | +1 412 |

*Source:* UK Department of Trade and Industry and Employment Department

\* In this table the value of earnings from tourism includes fares paid to UK carriers in respect of international transport and the value of earnings from civil aviation and sea transport excludes them.

† Includes expenditure of overseas visitors in the Channel Islands.

# 1.3 Leisure, tourism and demographic change

**Develops knowledge and understanding of the following element:**

1 Describe the scale and contexts of the leisure and tourism industry

**Supports development of the following core skills:**

Communication level 3: Take part in discussions; Application of number level 3: Interpret and present mathematical data (Task 1)

Communication level 3: Take part in discussions (Task 2)

Leisure and tourism statistics are important to industry in helping to evaluate people's current habits and predict what they might do in the future. To make even reasonably accurate predictions will often need figures covering a number of years. Sometimes, however, a single year's figures can provide some useful indicators to those involved in the research and planning of new projects in leisure and tourism.

Table 5 below looks at tourism activity in relation to three different ways of dividing the population: by age, by social class, and by the regions in which people live.

## Table 5 Demographic profile of UK tourism in UK1990

| | Total trips | Holiday trips | | Visits to friends and relatives non-holiday | Business and work | Adult population of UK |
| | | Short (1-3 nights) | Long (4+nights) | | | |
|---|---|---|---|---|---|---|
| **Age** | | | | | | |
| All trips to UK (age 15 and over) | 100 % | 100 % | 100 % | 100 % | 100 % | 100 % |
| 15–24 | 21 | 23 | 13 | 35 | 13 | 20 |
| 25–34 | 22 | 24 | 21 | 20 | 28 | 17 |
| 35–44 | 22 | 23 | 23 | 14 | 29 | 17 |
| 45–54 | 13 | 13 | 12 | 9 | 20 | 13 |
| 55–64 | 11 | 10 | 14 | 9 | 7 | 13 |
| 65+ | 11 | 6 | 17 | 13 | 2 | 19 |
| **Social class** | | | | | | |
| All trips to UK (age 15 and over) | 100 % | 100 % | 100 % | 100 % | 100 % | 100 % |
| AB: professional/managerial | 30 | 32 | 25 | 27 | 44 | 17 |
| C1: clerical/supervisory | 27 | 26 | 24 | 31 | 29 | 22 |
| C2: skilled manual | 25 | 25 | 28 | 23 | 20 | 29 |
| DE: unskilled/pensioners, etc. | 18 | 16 | 23 | 20 | 7 | 32 |
| **Region of residence** | | | | | | |
| All trips to UK (including children) | 100 % | 100 % | 100 % | 100 % | 100 % | 100 % |
| North | 6 | 8 | 6 | 6 | 6 | 5 |
| Yorkshire/Humberside | 9 | 10 | 9 | 7 | 6 | 9 |
| North West | 10 | 9 | 11 | 10 | 10 | 11 |
| East Midlands | 8 | 8 | 10 | 8 | 7 | 7 |
| West Midlands | 10 | 10 | 10 | 10 | 9 | 9 |
| East Anglia | 3 | 2 | 3 | 3 | 4 | 3 |
| Greater London | 12 | 12 | 11 | 15 | 9 | 12 |
| South East (excluding Greater London) | 20 | 19 | 19 | 20 | 26 | 17 |
| South West | 9 | 7 | 8 | 12 | 11 | 8 |
| Scotland | 5 | 6 | 7 | 3 | 5. | 9 |
| Wales | 5 | 5 | 5 | 6 | 6 | 5 |
| Northern Ireland | 2 | 3 | 2 | 1 | 1 | 4 |

Based on the characteristics of UK resident adults who formed the basis of the sample survey.

**Your tasks**

1 Discuss what conclusions each of the following five individuals might reach after they had studied Table 5 carefully:

   **a)** the Marketing Manager of the Yorkshire and Humberside Tourist Board

   **b)** the developers of a business and conference centre planned for a site in the East Midlands region

   **c)** a new tour operator planning to specialise in coach trips for the over-60s

   **d)** a hotel manager based in East Anglia intending to market a new weekend break offer

   **e)** a research student writing a thesis on the subject of 'Transport, mobility and the extended family'.

2 Use published data to help you to compile a list of the most significant demographic changes in the United Kingdom in the last 20 years.

   Discuss the extent to which you think each of these changes has affected the following:

   - local authority leisure provision
   - the development of regional tourist attractions
   - the marketing of specific overseas destinations.

# 1.4 The economic impact of sport

**Develops knowledge and understanding of the following element:**

1    Describe the scale and contexts of the leisure and tourism industry

**Supports development of the following core skill:**

Communication level 3: Prepare written material (Tasks 1, 2, 3)

David Teasdale, writing in the December 1992 edition of Leisure Management, emphasised the point that 'the sports economy has grown faster than the UK economy as a whole'. The following article summarises the main issues which led him to this view:

There has long been agreement that sport has an impact on the economy but it has generally proved difficult to assess. One reason for this is the uncertainty about what to include in the definition of sport. Generally cinemas, theatres, night clubs and bingo halls would be excluded from any measurement of the income derived from sport and yet these venues might be used occasionally for events such as boxing or snooker tournaments. Another difficult area is gambling which, although it may not be regarded as a sport in itself, invariably depends on sporting events.

For economic purposes sport-related activity can be divided into a number of sectors:

- community participation
- professional sport
- hospitality

- sponsorship and advertising
- voluntary clubs and governing bodies
- central government
- local government
- overseas.

It was recently estimated that these sectors between them resulted in an annual total spend of £8.27 billion, or 1.7 per cent of the Gross Domestic Product.

*Circuit training room, St James' Court Hotel*

In 1990 over £9 billion was spent on sports-related items, some £3 billion of that sum being spent on gambling. Even after deducting the latter figure, the sum is still greater than that spent on menswear, electricity or furniture. This spending is made up of sports goods and equipment, sports clothing and footwear, and the costs of sports participation.

Sport also creates employment. Its growing influence can be judged by the fact that the number of jobs in sport has risen from 376 000 in 1985 to 467 000 in 1992. A quarter of these jobs are classified as professional and managerial, and a further 13 per cent as skilled manual. Men and women are employed in almost equal numbers.

The Government receives £3.56 billion from sport, derived from

- VAT
- income tax and National Insurance
- excise and betting duty
- corporation tax.

Profit-making sports businesses are required to pay corporation tax on their profits. In turn the Government spends £533 million on sport, some of this money going in grants to the Sports Council. Local councils spend over £1 billion on sport and sports facilities but they receive more than three quarters of this back in fees, rents and other income.

The revenue enjoyed by commercial sports clubs expanded by 47 per cent between 1985 and 1990. Much of this is due to increased participation, but there is also an element of clubs making more effort to maximise their earning potential through putting on special events and hiring their premises out to other users.

Future spending on sport may be affected by a number of variables, not the least of which is the state of the national economy. Spectators of professional sport may be influenced by the standards of comfort and safety developed by individual facilities. The emphasis placed by the education system on different types of fitness activity will in turn have a future economic impact. The extent of government funding of sport will remain a matter of debate for as long as demand continues to grow, alongside increases in government income from this source.

## Your tasks

1 The economic importance of sport in your region is to be measured. Write a precise definition of sport which would help its economic significance to be accurately assessed.

2 List the recent evidence you can find in your region for:
   a) spending on sports-related goods
   b) participation in sports activities
   c) attendance at sports events
   d) the creation of jobs through sport.

3 Use the evidence you have gathered to write a short report which outlines a strategy for the future development of sport in the region.

# 1.5 Career opportunities

**Develops knowledge and understanding of the following element:**
1   Describe the scale and contexts of the leisure and tourism industry

**Supports development of the following core skills:**
Communication level 3: Take part in discussions (Task 1)
Information technology level 3: Select and use formats for presenting information (Task 2)
Communication level 3: Prepare written material (Task 3)

Leisure and tourism is an industry which attracts a range of new entrants, including school leavers and graduates. At one time it had the reputation of offering only seasonal unskilled or semi-skilled employment, but it now clearly offers a broad range of skilled, supervisory and management roles.

## Your tasks

1 Use the information provided in the flow chart on page 10 to prepare a short talk about the career opportunities available in hotel work.

**2** List the personal qualities which might be thought appropriate for hotel work at semi-skilled, skilled, supervisory or management levels.

**3** Choose a working environment in leisure and tourism, other than a hotel, which offers a range of career opportunities. You might select from the following:
- heritage centre
- tour operator
- major theme park
- transport company
- museum
- arts complex.

Create a flow chart showing possible entry points into this area of work, the qualifications required at different levels, and the possible career development.

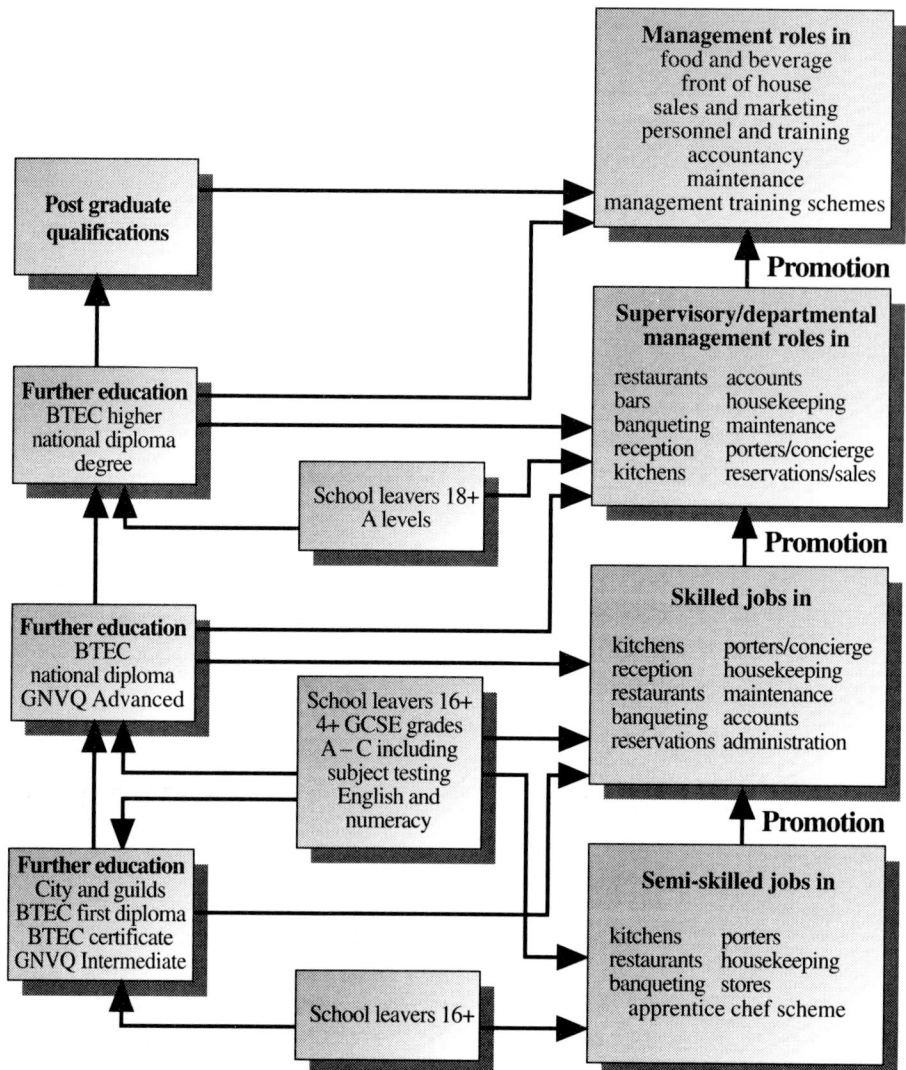

*Opportunities flow chart. An example of possible entry points into hotel-work*

| | |
|---|---|
| **Post graduate qualifications** | **Management roles in** food and beverage / front of house / sales and marketing / personnel and training / accountancy / maintenance / management training schemes |
| | **Promotion** |
| **Further education** BTEC higher national diploma degree | **Supervisory/departmental management roles in** restaurants / accounts / bars / housekeeping / banqueting / maintenance / reception / porters/concierge / kitchens / reservations/sales |
| **School leavers 18+** A levels | **Promotion** |
| **Further education** BTEC national diploma GNVQ Advanced | **Skilled jobs in** kitchens / porters/concierge / reception / housekeeping / restaurants / maintenance / banqueting / accounts / reservations / administration |
| **School leavers 16+** 4+ GCSE grades A – C including subject testing English and numeracy | **Promotion** |
| **Further education** City and guilds BTEC first diploma BTEC certificate GNVQ Intermediate | **Semi-skilled jobs in** kitchens / porters / restaurants / housekeeping / banqueting / stores / apprentice chef scheme |
| **School leavers 16+** | |

# 1.6 Employment in leisure and tourism: EC directives

**Develops knowledge and understanding of the following element:**
1    Describe the scale and contexts of the leisure and tourism industry

**Supports development of the following core skill:**
Communication level 3: Prepare written material (Tasks 1, 2)

The leisure and tourism industries are already being affected by labour **directives** from the European Community. These mainly cover areas such as health and safety, but they could be extended in the future to cover the rights of employees and guidelines for employers on redundancy and part-time employment.

Among the most important directives, many of which could become UK law in the future, are the following:

- a requirement to keep accurate lists of all staff on duty at any given time
- a defined minimum rest period each day and each week
- limits on the precise length of night shift work
- accurate record-keeping of all night shift work and all staff exceeding 48 hours' work a week
- stricter limits on the hours worked by 16–18-year-olds
- compulsory notification to part-time staff of any full-time posts which become available
- compulsory redundancy payments to anyone working between 5 and 18 hours a week

## Your tasks

1   Choose a single large leisure and tourism workplace. Find out how many people work there and explain the range and pattern of working hours of people with different roles within the organisation.

2   Write a short report explaining how this workplace would be affected if all the EC directives listed above became UK law in the near future.

# 1.7 The future of tourism in the countryside

**Develops knowledge and understanding of the following element:**
3    Investigate the variety of local services and products

**Supports development of the following core skills:**
Communication level 3: Take part in discussions (Task 1)
Communication level 3: Read and respond to written material and images (Task 2)
Communication level 3: Prepare written material (Task 3)

Many modern tourists are motivated by a strong need to escape from the urban environment. However, as greater numbers are drawn towards the most attractive landscapes, the quality and accessibility of the countryside come under threat. There is a great problem in trying to reconcile the need for leisure activity and the need to conserve the countryside. This is what the Countryside Commission has to say on the subject:

Providing facilities, such as car parks, toilets and shelter, for visitors to the countryside is often a costly task for recreation providers. Tourism operators could assist by allowing their own facilities to be used by a wider clientele beyond their existing customers. Such dual use of facilities would be a more effective use of resources and would be of mutual benefit because it would enhance the image of tourism businesses among potential future customers.

The Commission looks to the tourism industry to take the initiative in channelling some of its profits and visitor spending towards countryside conservation and recreation work. The Commission will assist by giving general advice on the most appropriate mechanisms and, in major schemes, will assist in the identification of projects and conservation organisations most able to carry out the work.

In addition, the contact that tourism businesses and their staff have with visitors means that they are well-placed to promote the values of conservation and considerate conduct among their guests, which is so important for the harmonious relationship between tourism and the environment. Studies have shown, however, that the contents of tourism literature often fail to give the visitor a better understanding or appreciation of the area promoted.

Here is a challenge: the creative and marketing talents of the tourism industry could be used to great effect in supporting conservation and sustainable tourism use of the countryside.

*Rydal Water, Cumbria*

The national network of **Tourism Information Centres** has great potential for acting as a much-needed focus for information on the countryside. Developing this potential would improve their usefulness to local people and tourists, alike.

Policies for tourism should be:

- the tourism industry should use its marketing activities, particularly leaflets and brochures, to stimulate a greater sense of care and understanding among visitors about the places they visit
- tourism operators should share their facilities more widely with visitors to the countryside
- the tourism industry should set up environmental funds, and other mechanisms, for attracting resources from visitors and tourism businesses into practical conservation and recreation work
- the development of tourism in the countryside should follow the Principles for Tourism in the Countryside endorsed by the Commission and the **English Tourist Board**.

### Your tasks

1  Draw up your own list of principles or guidelines which you think should apply to the further development of tourism in the countryside.
   Compare your own list with the suggestions made by others in the group and try to establish which ones you all agree on. Arrange these under a series of major headings. How do your ideas compare with those suggested by the English Tourist Board and The Countryside Commission in the extract quoted here?

2  Choose a countryside location which is known to appeal to tourists. Collect a selection of brochures and leaflets which promote its various attractions and which illustrate the range of facilities and services available.
   Study this tourist literature and evaluate it from two points of view:
   **a)**  How effectively does it give the visitor an understanding of the area promoted?
   **b)**  Does it contribute in any way to the conservation of the area?

3  Write a report summarising how the literature could contribute more to making sure that the area keeps its attractiveness.

# 1.8  Responding to different customer groups

**Develops knowledge and understanding of the following element:**
3      Investigate the variety of local services and products

**Supports development of the following core skills:**
Communication level 3: Take part in discussions (Task 1)
Communication level 3: Prepare written material (Task 2)

Tourist attractions are constantly seeking new ways of broadening their appeal. Advances in technology are increasingly seen as essential in achieving this. The Product Department of the English Tourist Board recently suggested four main reasons for this:

- the interaction offered by using technology encourages greater participation, increasing the visitor's experience and enjoyment
- interactive techniques promote learning and tie in with the trend in education towards learning by experience
- technological hardware is becoming cheaper
- people are becoming more familiar with technology, both in and out of the home.

Among the most recent developments are:

- simulated war games: participants use computer-controlled laser guns to eliminate their opponents from the game
- fairground rides which rely on simulated background scenery
- robotics and animatronics used in attractions like Rock Circus and the Museum of the Moving Image.

The area which seems to have the greatest future potential, however, is known as Virtual Reality, or VR. Participants enter a computer-generated three-dimensional world by means of a helmet and joystick control. Such systems could be used for educational purposes as well as for games. Museums could use the system to recreate scenes and events from the past. Combined with interactive techniques already in use, it could simplify the learning of theories and principles which learners otherwise find hard to grasp. This is assuming, of course, that you agree with the principle that we learn more effectively when the process is made enjoyable!

### Your tasks

1 Discuss the reasons why tourist attractions are increasingly making use of advanced technology.
2 Choose an example of a tourist attraction which appears to cater mainly for a specific age or interest group.
  Write a report outlining how using technology might mean that the attraction could respond to the expectations and needs of a broader range of customers

# 1.9 Swindon: tourism and the local economy

### Develops knowledge and understanding of the following element:
3    Investigate the variety of local services and products

### Supports development of the following core skills:
Communication level 3: Take part in discussions; Read and respond to written material and images (Task 1)
Communication level 3: Prepare written material (Task 2)

We have long been used to brochures and advertisements praising the merits of seaside resorts and rural beauty spots, but now less obvious tourist destinations are beginning to seek greater economic benefit from tourism. A good example is Swindon, for many years known mainly as a railway town. The following extract introduces the town's Visitors' Guide:

Swindon offers you the best of both worlds: a wide choice of town and country attractions, combining all the benefits of a 'city break' with the chance to explore rural England at its most appealing.

Despite its young and modern image, Swindon is not a new town. For nearly 150 years it was one of the world's great railway centres. Today you can savour the heritage of Brunel's Great Western Railway at the Railway Museum and the unique Railway Village, one of the earliest and most perfect examples of a planned workers' estate. In the Old Town there is an even earlier Swindon to be discovered. Many fine buildings recall the original hill-top market town which was mentioned in the Domesday Book. At its heart is The Lawn, a 50-acre park which was the home of the Goddard family, Swindon's 'Lords of the Manor' for over 300 years. In sharp contrast, Swindon's new business parks provide some celebrated examples of contemporary architecture – striking symbols of Swindon's place at the fore-front of the hi-tech revolution.

Superb leisure facilities mean Swindon is great for families. The exciting Domebusters water-slides at the Oasis, ice-skating at the Link Centre, ten-pin bowling at the Superbowl or the latest movies at the 7-screen cinema will all keep the children happy while you can take time to explore one of the many historic houses nearby or enjoy a leisurely cream tea. Top class evening entertainment is provided at the Wyvern Theatre and the Town's other arts venues, while a wide range of restaurants and nightclubs cater for all ages and tastes.

Less than an hour from London by High Speed Train and easily accessible from all parts of Britain, Swindon is at the centre of England's finest countryside and most famous attractions. Whether for a short break or a longer holiday, Swindon has all the ingredients you need: touring, walking, sporting, cycling, living it up or just winding down!

## Your tasks

1  Use a good road atlas to locate tourist attractions within easy reach of Swindon and the main access routes to them. You might include the following: Bath, the Vale of the White Horse at Uffington, Avebury Stone Circle, the Railway Centre at Didcot, the Thames Valley, the Kennet and Avon Canal, the Cotswolds, Oxford.
   Discuss the numbers and type of visitors each of these locations might attract, how much economic benefit the local community is likely to gain from these visits, and whether their nearness to Swindon is an overall advantage or disadvantage to those trying to market Swindon as a tourist attraction.

2  Read the following information about how to get to Swindon and then study the map overleaf.
   - **Road:** Swindon is served by the M4 motorway, Junctions 15 (East) and 16 (West) and the A4361, A361, A420, A345, and A419 trunk roads. London is only 90 minutes by road, Bristol 40 minutes. Regular National Express coach services run from London and other major towns and cities
   - **Air:** from London Heathrow it is quicker to reach Swindon than Central London itself! The M4 provides a direct route from Heathrow, while rail travellers can take a fast coach to Reading to connect with a High Speed Train. From Gatwick the M25 connects with the M4, while Bristol, Cardiff and Southampton airports are all within easy reach
   - **Rail:** Swindon is only 50 minutes from London by High Speed Train. The 125

**Legend:**

1. Tourist Office/Brunel Centre
2. Broome Manor Golf Complex
3. Coate Water
4. County Ground Complex
5. Dorcan Pool & Squash Court
6. GWR Museum
7. Highworth Recreation Centre
8. Link Centre
9. Lydiard Country Park
10. Health Hydro & Baths
11. Museum & Art Gallery
12. Oasis Leisure Centre
13. Wroughton Sports Centre
14. Wyvern Theatre
15. Delta Tennis Centre
16. Train Station

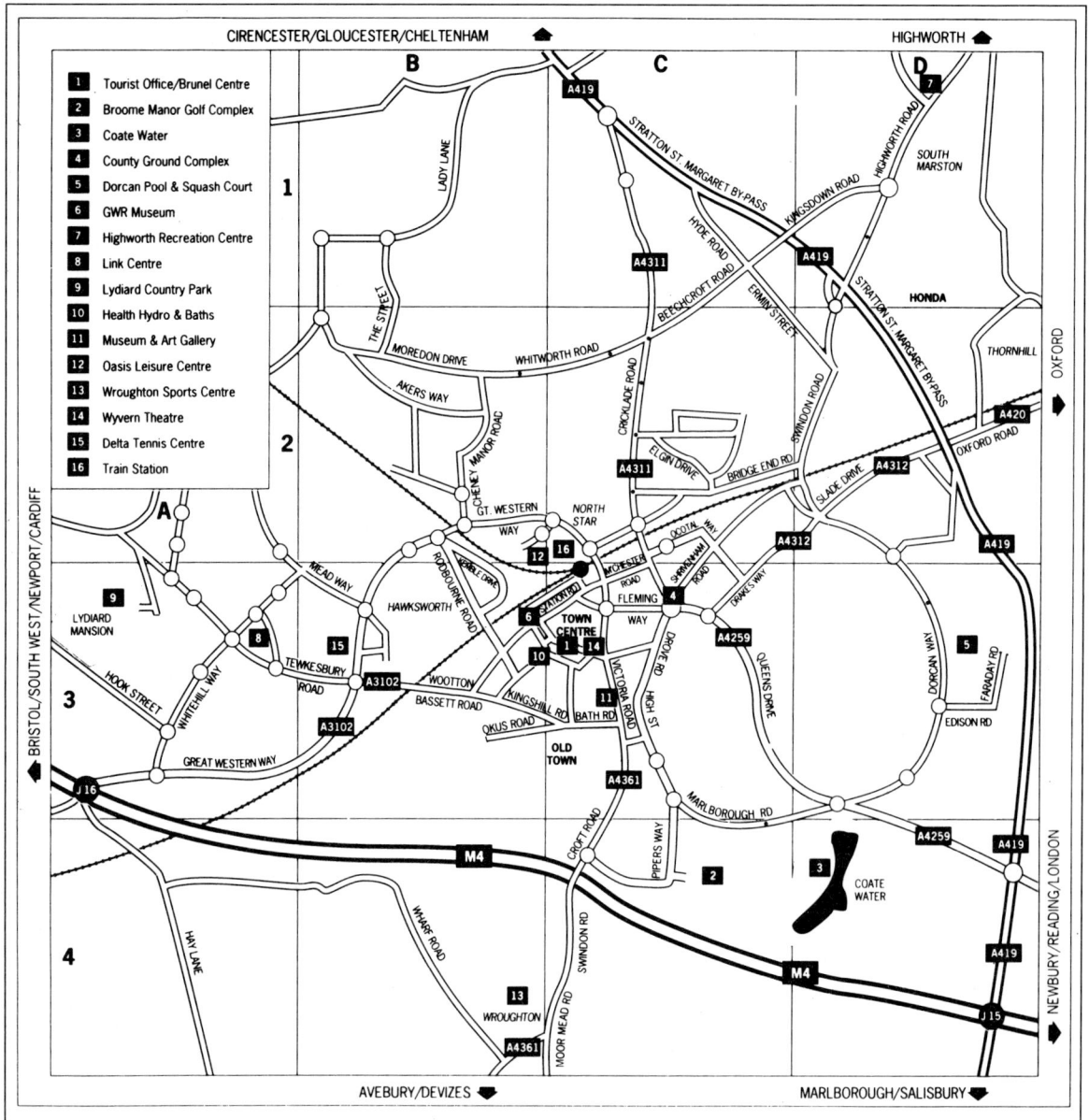

*Swindon town centre*

service also links Swindon with Bath, Bristol, and South Wales, while other services provide easy access to the Midlands and North.

Find two kinds of leisure or tourism provision which the town currently lacks. Assume that no development land is available in the map grid squares B3 and C3. Suggest two different possible sites for each development.

Compare the possible access routes and the populations of some of the towns from which you might expect to attract visitors. Write two short reports explaining, in each case, which site would be more likely to bring income into the town.

# 1.10 The National Trust: sources of funding

**Develops knowledge and understanding of the following element:**

4     Identify sources of income for different types of leisure and tourism operation.

**Supports development of the following core skills:**

Communication level 3: Read and respond to written material and images (Task 1)
Communication level 3: Take part in discussions (Task 2)

Tourists who are fond of the countryside, and in particular of country houses, owe much to the National Trust. The Trust manages and conserves much important landscape and many historic properties. Keeping up this work demands extensive funds. These are drawn from a variety of sources. The following extract, adapted from the National Trust's Annual Report of 1991, describes how the organisation gained and managed its financial resources:

During 1991 the Chancellor of the Exchequer raised the rate of VAT by 2½ per cent which resulted in a loss to the Trust of some £800 000. Income from **deeds of covenant** on members' subscriptions was affected by a change in the Inland Revenue's rules which now requires covenants to last for a minimum of four years. This made it difficult to retain the proportion of members willing to sign them.

*National Trust land at Ravenscar, North Yorkshire*

Despite these problems the Trust succeeded in increasing its profits through the trading

activities of National Trust Enterprises Limited. Though there was a decline in the number of paying visitors and in agricultural rents, income from **legacies** reached a record level. Membership grew by almost 6 per cent during the year and non-agricultural rents increased by 7 per cent. The huge growth in membership over the last 25 years makes it unlikely that it will increase further. This has also resulted in a reduction of paying visitors to individual properties, since membership of the Trust gives free entry to these.

National Trust Enterprises Limited produced a **turnover** of more than £30 million, mainly through its retailing, catering and holiday cottage activities. However, such enterprises require new investment each year. Catering outlets may need funds to ensure that they comply with the provisions of the new Food Safety Act. Some of the Trust's shops were refitted and a number of new ones were opened. Approximately 200 products were introduced, including new toiletries, conserves, home fragrances and pottery. The company offered a number of specialist holidays within the United Kingdom, as well as cruises to Norway and the Rhine.

The Trust received funding from a number of companies during 1991. British Gas became their largest sponsor to date by providing £500 000 over five years to support the work of the Trust's wardens. Barclays Bank are providing £350 000 over six years to support the Young National Trust Theatre. Other sponsors supported events such as concerts or firework displays at individual National Trust properties.

Other important sources of income include **charitable trusts** which increasingly recognise the direct social impact of many of the Trust's projects, particularly those which create employment, help to maintain communities, or make special provision for young people or those with disabilities. Appeals associated with particular regions, such as the Snowdonia Appeal, did well during the year, and new appeals for work in the Yorkshire Moors and Dales and on the South Downs were launched in the autumn. Regional projects also benefited from contributions from the European Regional Development Fund.

The extensive programme of **capital works** carried out by the Trust is very dependent on **bequests.** These are normally used in the year after receipt either for major restoration projects at existing properties or to buy and endow new properties. £23.5 million came to the Trust in 1991 as a result of legacies. Some of these specified how and where the money was to be used, but the remainder will largely be spent on the 1992 Capital Programme which includes activities such as:

- building restoration
- farm buildings
- landscape conservation
- visitors and access
- drains and sewers
- fire and security.

In terms of future needs, the Trust has identified £125 million worth of capital works which need to be completed on its properties in the next five years. As a high proportion of the National Trust's funds is committed to specific purposes, especially the **endowment** of properties, it will have to go on increasing its income if it is to complete the identified capital works, improve its standard of property management, and rescue important new properties.

## Your tasks

1 Answer the following questions, some of which may require research:

 a) What is VAT? When is there no requirement to pay VAT?

 b) What is a deed of covenant? Why might the Inland Revenue's change of rules make National Trust members less willing to sign these?

 c) What reasons might you suggest to explain the National Trust's thirteen-fold increase in membership over the last 25 years?

 d) What sort of products can be bought in National Trust shops? What reasons can you give to explain why the Trust concentrates on this particular range of products?

 e) What do you think the companies who sponsor various aspects of the National Trust's work get in return for their investment?

 f) What does endow mean? What specific activities might the National Trust have to undertake in order to endow a new property?

2 List as many arguments as you can think of for and against the following points of view:

 a) 'The name, National Trust, doesn't give a clear enough message to the public about what the organisation actually does.'

 b) 'The National Trust should be wholly funded by central government.'

 c) 'The principles of profit-making and the principles of conservation are essentially incompatible.'

 d) 'Instead of spending money restoring historic houses, more funds should be directed towards building much-needed new houses.'

With a partner, discuss the strength and weakness of the arguments you have listed.

# 1.11 Raising finance for projects

**Develops knowledge and understanding of the following element:**
4 Identify sources of income for different types of leisure and tourism operation.

**Supports development of the following core skills:**
Communication level 3: Read and respond to written material and images (Task 1)
Information technology level 3: Select and use formats for presenting information (Task 2)

Anyone thinking of starting up a caravan park, converting a house into holiday apartments or developing any other leisure or tourism scheme must first of all make sure that they have sufficient finance. They must also be sure that there is enough demand for the product or service to:

- pay the costs of this finance
- provide them with an adequate income.

Banks will lend money for projects, but only if they are satisfied that the proposition is viable. The major banks advise potential borrowers to prepare a business plan. The plan should cover a number of important areas:

- the scheme's objectives
- its potential market
- the nature of the product or service being offered
- the intended pricing policy
- the supplies, premises and equipment needed
- any extra personnel to be employed
- the expertise and experience of the proposer of the project
- the marketing plans
- the book-keeping and recording system to be used.

Perhaps the most difficult part of the business plan is estimating accurately the level of sales which can be achieved. A hotel planning an extension will have to calculate what rate of room occupancy it can reasonably expect to achieve and what it would require in order to break even. **Cash flow** is also important: a travel agent specialising in business travel may find itself waiting for accounts to be settled by its customers at the end of a quarterly period and not having sufficient cash to pay its weekly and monthly bills.

There is plenty of professional advice available to people planning new projects. In addition to the banks themselves, local trade associations, Regional Tourist Boards, and national organisations like the Rural Development Commission may be able to offer guidance and opinions about the likely **viability** of the proposal. In some regions there may be grants available for developments which meet specified criteria. These are more common in areas of declining industry, in those facing depopulation and in inner city areas needing **regeneration.**

Before banks will agree to lend money, they need to be sure that businesses can cope with unexpected setbacks. If the cost of building extra hotel rooms proves greater than expected, they may wish to know whether the hotel owner would raise prices (and risk attracting fewer guests), or whether they would reduce costs by dismissing staff (and risk a lower level of service). Since hotels often depend on repeat business, it would be counter-productive to cut the costs of a new development if facilities or services then appeared to the guests to be inferior.

Most banks lending large sums for business projects will ask for some kind of **security.** The value of the security will need to be higher than the amount lent, with a safety margin between the two sums so that both parties have some degree of protection if things go wrong. Many borrowers will offer **freehold** land or property as security against the loan, others will **remortgage** property to raise cash to invest in a business scheme. As hotel owners have found recently, remortgaging property can harm a business if property values fall sharply and the renegotiated mortgage stands at a higher value than the **market value** of the property. Machinery or equipment is rarely accepted as security.

Banks will probably expect business borrowers to invest an amount from their own funds to match the sum the bank is lending them. This is to show that the borrower is committed to making a success of the project, as well as limiting the extent of the bank's loss if the scheme fails. Most lenders will also insist on the borrower taking out an insurance policy, so that the loan is repaid if the borrower dies or is unable to work because of an accident or ill health.

The structure of loan repayments may vary considerably too.

- The interest to be repaid may be at a fixed rate, or may vary according to changes in the bank's **base rate.**

- Special terms may be available for business starters which postpone all repayments for an agreed period while the business is getting established.

A government Loan Guarantee Scheme will in some circumstances guarantee most of a loan in return for a **premium payment** of 2.5 per cent of the guaranteed amount.

## Your tasks

1 Write definitions of the following words or phrases used in the passage above: viable break even    cash flow    security    remortgage    base rate

2 You decide to set up a new business making and selling small souvenirs of the region in which you live.

Draw up the first draft of a business plan which will enable you to do the following things:

- decide whether the business will work
- identify the income and expenditure involved
- monitor the progress of the business
- provide your bank with sufficient background for them to judge whether and how they might help you.

# Unit 2  Maintaining health, safety and security

## 2.1  Health and safety: Chessington World of Adventures

**Develops knowledge and understanding of the following element:**
1    Report on the health, safety and security arrangements in a facility

**Supports development of the following core skill:**
Communication level 3: Prepare written material (Tasks 1, 2)

Over a million visitors and a thousand employees visited or worked at Chessington World of Adventures in 1991. Given the presence of wild animals and of a range of mechanical rides, health and safety are critical factors in the management and development of the attraction.

Chessington Zoo started life in 1931 as a small private collection of animals. Pearsons plc bought the expanded collection in 1975 and the group expanded its interests in the leisure industry by buying Madame Tussauds in 1978. A multi-million pound investment transformed Chessington into a theme park, although the collection of animals was largely retained. The attraction opened for the first time as Chessington World of Adventures in 1987.

The mixed nature of the site means that there are five maintenance areas involved, all of which carry a health and safety responsibility:
- buildings maintenance
- gardens maintenance
- rides maintenance
- vehicle maintenance
- site cleaning.

It also means that plumbers, carpenters, labourers, engineers, electricians and cleaners are all employed, as well as the employees working directly with the public.

Chessington World of Adventures Limited has a number of responsibilities under the Health and Safety at Work Act (1974).
- Safe and healthy working conditions must be provided for employees, including training to enable them to carry out their duties safely and efficiently.
- Safety devices and protective equipment must be available and their use must be supervised.

● The company consults its own employees, either individually or through their representatives, to make sure that safe and healthy working practices continue to be used.

To carry out these responsibilities at Chessington, a Health and Safety Committee has been appointed. Its objectives are to turn the legislation into safe practice by developing safe operating systems, safe working places and safe usage and storage of equipment. For these things to be done effectively the objectives must be communicated through training, supervision and written instruction.

It is not, however, only the company itself which has legal responsibilities. The Act also applies to employees who are required to co-operate with company safety policies and recommendations. This may be by wearing appropriate protective clothing, reporting hazards, or helping in investigating accidents.

At Chessington the General Manager is answerable to the Board for the safety performance of the attraction. Day-to-day responsibilities are delegated to managers and supervisors. They must apply safety rules such as checking equipment, investigating accidents and inspecting repairs. They must also ensure that all staff are familiar with the specific instructions which apply in different

*The Vampire, the hanging rollercoaster at Chessington World of Adventures*

areas of the site and in the event of any emergency. Specific instructions cover procedures in the case of fire or an animal escaping. Training in the operation of fire equipment and emergency procedures is undertaken by the Safety Officer and the appropriate departmental manager. There are strict rules about entering animal cages or enclosures and, except in the case of an emergency, animal keepers must give their consent for any other member of staff to enter. If an accident should happen, staff are trained to know from where first aid can be requested and who to contact if outside help is needed. An investigation will be held to find out the cause of the accident and how to avoid any repetition.

Materials and machinery can be hazardous and great care is taken at Chessington to ensure that both are safe. New machinery is thoroughly tested before it is used. If new materials are potentially hazardous, instruction sheets on the safest way to use them are prepared and circulated.

Ride safety is particularly important. A practice similar to the pre-flight checks operated by airlines is used to ensure that rides are always in safe working order. A form known as a DID (Daily Inspection Document) indicates the nature of any repair or maintenance work carried out and creates an accurate record of the performance of machinery. New rides are only bought from reputable constructors; Chessington's engineers will recommend specifications of their own if they think a particular design has any potential risk, however remote. Drivers of the rides undergo thorough training and must pass written and practical tests before they are allowed to operate the rides. This training also includes learning how to diagnose potential mechanical faults and also how to carry out safe evacuation procedures.

Employees' specific responsibilities include:

- vehicle drivers keeping within speed limits
- catering staff doing everything to ensure the highest standards of hygiene: any suggestions which they might have for improving safety are encouraged
- employees working with the animals have to be aware of the dangers of wounds, especially where the animals may be carriers of diseases like hepatitis B. They have to be particularly careful when animals are being treated, especially if they are being injected with powerful anaesthetics!

Environmental Health Officers are charged with administering the 1981 Zoo Licensing Act. In particular this involves checking that the standards maintained in the cages are acceptable.

As with many things dangerous to health, prevention is often better than cure. Chessington's safety policy emphasises good organisation and management:

- giving detailed attention to proper storage procedures
- inspecting machine safety devices regularly
- servicing animal cages regularly
- competent personnel regularly examining and testing electrical equipment and wiring.

Anything found to be defective has to be withdrawn from service until faults are put right, even if this means stopping a popular ride in the middle of a busy summer's day.

## Your tasks

1 In what ways might the visiting public contribute to accidents at zoos or leisure parks with mechanical rides?
    Suggest a number of ways of trying to reduce the possibility of accidents involving visitors.
    What are the practical issues which attraction managers would have to confront before deciding whether each of your suggestions was worth investing in?

2 Specific safety instructions are to be issued to employees at a theme park like Chessington. Make some notes which could be used as a basis for these instructions for each of the following groups:
    - gardeners
    - site cleaners
    - vehicle maintenance staff.

# 2.2  Health and safety: caves open to the public

**Develops knowledge and understanding of the following element:**

I    Report on the health, safety and security arrangements in a facility

**Supports development of the following core skill:**

Communication level 3: Prepare written material (Tasks 1, 2, 3, 4)

When people are inside buildings, for business or leisure, many issues concerning health and safety will be similar. For example, the occupants will need as much protection as possible in the event of fire or accidents. Natural attractions like caves are not designed to be occupied by people. They present Health and Safety Officers, as well as the companies which manage the sites, with a number of distinctive challenges.

The shape of the cave itself may present some obvious hazards. The height of some parts of the roof may be below average head height and there may be sharp, jagged stones in both the roof and walls. Caves are often dimly lit, especially in the narrower passages, and clear guidance is essential if injuries are to be avoided. This means not only indicating where visitors should lower their heads but also pointing out accurately the distance they should step before standing upright again. The ground underfoot may also be uneven. Steps have often been cut into rock and the height of each step can differ. Caves have often been created as a result of river systems cutting through rock formations and pathways may therefore be damp and slippery. Guides will need to point out any particularly difficult spots, and, where possible, handrails will need to be fitted to make steps and slopes easier to negotiate.

Lighting is important: a party of visitors trying to find its way out of a series of caves in complete darkness would be at serious risk of injury. At Wookey Hole Cave, in Somerset, lighting is fixed a foot above floor level so that visitors can see where they are walking. Other lights are fixed into the walls of the caves in order to illuminate their most interesting features. Each guide carries a torch and there is a back-up lighting system which can operate independently for up to eight hours in the event of mains failure. There are telephones at regular intervals through the cave system so that guides can contact the surface should they need to do so.

*The Great Hall, Wookey Hole Caves*

Most underground cave systems, natural or the result of industrial mining, contain areas considered unsafe for the general public. These may be steep shafts, for example, or areas of deep water. Visitors are generally kept away from these by strong mesh fencing and sometimes spoken and written warnings as well.

Most cave systems open to the public generally have a natural safety advantage if they contain bottlenecks, which may be narrow passages, or single track bridges built across chasms or underground lakes and rivers. Visitors have to move slowly and carefully through these parts of the cave system.

One fairly new issue which the owners of caves open to the public have had to consider is the possible presence of radon gas. This radioactive material exists naturally underground and in some circumstances has been known to build up to concentration levels which need to be monitored. There are already regulations governing the levels of radon gas found in mines. These are quite strict, since dust acts as a carrier of the gas and its concentration may be higher than in caves where the type of rock formation makes its presence a possibility.

The Health and Safety Executive is currently discussing with the British Association of Show Caves how to set levels for caves. Readings are taken regularly and there is a system of grading them.

- At the first level the Health and Safety Executive has to be notified.
- At the second the public has to be made aware.
- At the third level access has to be restricted.

However, the actual risk to an individual visitor is thought to be extremely low; much less than, say, exposure to sunlight. Guides will of course spend much more time underground than individual visitors, but at Wookey Hole, for example, it is estimated that each guide spends 1000 hours underground and the safety level is set at 6000 hours. Guides will sometimes carry equipment to monitor radon levels, since these vary according to temperature and humidity. Good ventilation also keeps the air clear. The cave system open to the public leaves the hillside at a different point from the entrance, which means that the ventilation system draws air in at one end of the system and expels it at the other.

Nine chambers at Wookey Hole are now open to the public, but a further sixteen were discovered between 1948 and 1976. These are only accessible to divers with breathing equipment and all visits are controlled by the British Cave Diving Group. Visibility underwater is limited, particularly once the mud on the bottom has been disturbed. A bright orange rope runs through the chambers, some of which are very narrow, in order to help divers to find their way back. Divers who want to reach the last chamber have to attach breathing equipment to their thighs so that they can squeeze through the narrower gaps. At the end of the system there is an abyss which descends more than 200 feet. Such a descent would require a special breathing mixture and regular stops for decompression on the ascent.

## Your tasks

1 Write the text of a notice to be displayed at the entrance to Wookey Hole Caves, intended to ensure the safety of visitors.

2 Identify the risks which you think visitors to each of the following five types of natural attraction might face:

- cliffs (for example Beachy Head, Land's End)
- beaches (for example Blackpool, Margate, Newquay)
- mountains (for example Snowdonia)
- moors (for example Exmoor, North Yorkshire Moors)
- lakes (for example Windermere, Loch Ness).

3  For each type of natural attraction, list the risks in rank order, beginning with what you think is the most dangerous and working down to the least serious.

4  Choose a specific natural attraction which falls into one of the five categories listed in Task 2. Write a report explaining the possible health and safety risks for visitors to your chosen site. You should include proposals of measures intended to reduce the level of those risks to a minimum

# 2.3  Injury risks in the catering industry

**Develops knowledge and understanding of the following element:**

I  Report on the health, safety and security arrangements in a facility

**Supports the development of the following core skill:**

Communication level 3: Use images to illustrate points made in writing and discussion (Tasks 1, 2)

Catering might seem to be a much safer occupation than general manufacturing, but the following article taken from *Caterer and Hotelkeeper* suggests that the risks are higher than you might suppose:

Delegates at last week's Institution of Environmental Health Officers annual conference in Bournemouth heard that in 1990/1 three people were killed, 603 badly hurt and 3477 were forced to take more than three days off work because of catering accidents.

But although the incidence of 'over three-day' accidents, for example, was relatively small, at 60.3 per 100 000 employees, the number of mishaps reported was very low, at just 15 per cent. This compared with an incidence rate of 137.7 per 100 000 in general manufacturing, but a reporting level of 30 per cent.

John Bouckley, principal inspector in the Health and Safety Executive's local authority unit, said catering seemed, at first glance, to be only half as dangerous as heavy industry. But because of massive under-reporting a comparative figure could be drawn of 120 accidents per 100 000.

'When you look at the figures for incidence rates, it looks as if catering is a safe industry,' he said, 'but the information must be treated with caution. It might be that catering is not one of the low-risk industries but is up with general manufacturing.'

He said the HSE was now looking at how legislation could be simplified to improve reporting levels. Although not all accidents were reported, Mr Bouckley said that statistics could help to identify areas of high risk.

Slips caused 1069 'over three-day' injuries, 804 of them as a result of manual handling, 552 due to harmful substances and 449 from being struck by a falling object.

The hotel and catering industry has shown the largest growth in accidents over the last five years, but despite the hazards, Mr Bouckley admitted that food safety attracted more enforcement kudos than health and safety. However, this situation is set to change with the introduction of new EC health and safety regulations due to come into force on 1st January 1993. These will force new approaches on general health and safety management, equipment safety, workplace conditions, manual handling of loads, personal protective equipment and display screens.

*A chef at work*

### Your tasks

1 Draw a floor plan of a kitchen used by a restaurant or a catering service.
Mark on the plan the most common movements of personnel working in the kitchen. Identify and mark any specific areas of the kitchen where you think people should take particular care.
Make a general list of the potential hazards facing the staff using this kitchen and group these into two categories: major risks and minor risks.

2 Design a poster, to be placed in a prominent place on the kitchen wall, to illustrate a code of safe practice which should be followed by all personnel working in the kitchen.

# 2.4  Health and safety legislation: legionnaire's disease

**Develops knowledge and understanding of the following element:**
1    Report on the health, safety and security arrangements in a facility

**Supports development of the following core skills:**
Communication level 3: Take part in discussions (Task 1)
Application of number level 3: Gather and process data (Task 2)
Communication level 3: Take part in discussions (Task 3)

The Health and Safety at Work Act of 1974 lays down rules of behaviour and conditions in the workplace to make it safe for workers, visitors and customers. The employer is responsible for training staff in the use of safe and hygienic working methods. There must also be a company Health and Safety Policy available for staff to read.

This Act has general applications, but individual workplaces may require more specific regulations. For example, some of the hazards involved in working with particular materials are covered by the Control of Substances Hazardous to Health Regulations (1988). In addition there are a number of Codes of Practice which are approved by the Health and Safety Commission on behalf of the Government. These cover specific health and safety risks; for example there is one dealing with the prevention or control of legionellosis, the family of bacteria which includes the one responsible for legionnnaire's disease.

Since legionnaire's disease is transmitted through the inhalation of water droplets, care must be taken wherever water is sprayed, bubbled or makes impact with hard surfaces. Legionella bacteria grow most rapidly in water temperatures between 20 and 45 degrees Celsius, although the organisms can remain dormant in cool water. Their growth is also more likely where there is sediment or organic material in the water. Some kinds of pipework and water fittings are more likely to be colonised by the bacteria, and layers of slime can be a barrier to successful chemical treatment.

Large poorly maintained air conditioning systems present the highest risk of spreading legionnaire's disease, but there is also some risk in spa baths and pools. In spa baths warm water is constantly recirculated, often through high velocity jets or with the injection of air to agitate the water. Between each use the water is filtered and chemically treated. Avoiding the danger of infection means frequent cleaning of filters and regular water treatment. Whirlpool baths are safer installations in leisure centres, mainly because the water is discharged after each separate use.

The main methods of preventing the spread of legionella are:
- carefully regulating water temperatures
- avoiding water stagnation
- choosing materials which do not encourage bacterial growth
- cleaning systems regularly
- where appropriate, treating water with chemicals
- ensuring that all water systems are well maintained.

Other leisure and tourism facilities which could represent high risk areas if they failed to comply with the regulations are swimming pools, jacuzzis and fountains. These, as well as all hot water systems, need to be regularly checked and cleaned. Failure to do this can lead to prosecution.

Codes of practice place specific responsibility on employers. In the case of a health risk such as legionnaire's disease they would be required to do the following:
- identify and assess the sources of risk
- prepare schemes to prevent or control the risks
- implement and manage precautions
- keep records of the precautions taken.

The responsibilities of manufacturers and suppliers of equipment are also laid down. Inspections to check that the codes are being followed are carried out either by Health and Safety Executive inspectors or by local authority public health inspectors.

### Your tasks

1  You are asked to draw up a code of practice for the management of the following:
   - a travelling fairground
   - a canoe club
   - a mobile children's library
   - a pony-trekking centre.

   Discuss the specific health and safety risks which you would need to deal with for each facility.

2  Visit a sports or leisure centre and collect evidence of the following:
   - potential hazards relating to the building itself
   - potential hazards relating to equipment
   - potential hazards relating to other users
   - the level of staff supervision of activities
   - the number and quality of safety notices displayed for the benefit of users
   - signs relating to emergency procedures.

3  Prepare an induction talk for new employees at your chosen centre on health and safety practice. The talk should indicate:
   - what training will be necessary
   - what level of competence each new employee will have to reach before they are allowed to operate unsupervised
   - how this competence will be assessed.

# 2.5  The work of an EHO

**Develops knowledge and understanding of the following element:**
1    Report on the health, safety and security arrangements in a facility

**Supports the development of the following core skills:**
Communication level 3: Take part in discussions (Task 1)
Application of number level 3: Gather and process data (Task 2)

The Health and Safety Executive is responsible for workplace safety in places like factories, farms, mines, fairgrounds, railways and building sites; local government Environmental Health Officers, however, currently cover health and safety issues in shops, offices, hotels, restaurants and leisure centres.

One of the many responsibilities of an Environmental Health Officer is the prevention of risk either in or near the workplace. The Health and Safety at Work Act (1974) and the regulations to enforce it mean that an EHO has to check that both those involved in commercial activities and those living nearby are not exposed to risk. This means checking that the following areas of the workplace reach the accepted standards:

- cleanliness
- temperature
- ventilation
- lighting
- washing and toilet facilities
- safety of machinery and materials.

If an employee is injured in a non-industrial workplace the EHO is responsible for investigating the accident. The employer is responsible for ensuring that machinery is not dangerous and that ventilation and lighting are sufficient for tasks to be performed safely. If the EHO decides that working conditions are not satisfactory, he or she can invoke the law to make sure that improvements are made.

Food service is a critical part of the leisure and tourism industries, and it is the Environmental Health Officer's job to ensure that food supplies are clean and safe. They have to check that all stages of food production, from slaughter or harvesting right through to public consumption, do not allow dangerous impurities to appear. Hotels, restaurants, public houses, food shops and mobile food outlets are inspected to see that they are not carrying contaminated food. An EHO will investigate complaints about bad food or dirty eating places and, if it is found necessary, take legal proceedings against the offenders. They will also attempt to trace the origin of any reported cases of food poisoning, suggesting how risks of any future outbreaks from the same source can be reduced.

Environmental Health Officers also monitor cases of air pollution and excessive noise. For example, people living near airports may suffer considerable disruption to their daily lives as a result of aircraft noise. The EHO will be able to advise them whether or not they qualify for a local authority grant to insulate their homes against the noise. He or she may also advise on planning applications for leisure developments, such as sports stadia or night clubs, where the local residents fear that noise will increase to the point where it threatens their normal daily lives.

Travel may also be responsible for small scale but serious health risks. Occasionally people who have been abroad return with infectious diseases. The EHO, having taken specialist medical advice, may need to ensure that the victim is kept in isolation so that other lives are not put at risk. The EHO will also carry out health checks at ports. The officer looks particularly at imported foodstuffs to see that they are free of vermin or other infestations. The EHO has legal power to rid premises of pests such as rats, mice and insects.

Environmental Health Officers have a number of smaller, specialist duties which particularly concern leisure and tourism:
- to check that water supplies and swimming pools are clean and wholesome
- to inspect and grant licences to centres where there are live animals, for example equestrian centres
- to check retail premises, including those catering specifically for tourists, to ensure that their products are safe and hygienic
- to check the standards at camping and caravan sites before issuing the licence the sites need to operate.

Some EHOs also have responsibilities for the standards of accommodation offered on canal and other leisure boats.

**Your tasks**

1 List the ways in which a new camping and/or caravan site might affect a rural environment.

Discuss each possible effect under the following headings:

**a)** how serious you think it will be

**b)** the possible measures which could be taken to counter it

**c)** the likely cost and viability of each of the proposed measures.

2 The owner of an intended new camping and/or caravan site needs to assess whether they have fully considered all the relevant health and safety issues. Draw up a questionnaire which will help them to do this.

# 2.6 Preventing business crime

### Develops knowledge and understanding of the following element:

1 Report on the health, safety and security arrangements in a facility

### Supports the development of the following core skills:

Communication level 3: Read and respond to written material and images (Task 1)

Communication level 3: Prepare written material (Task 2)

Business crime prevention can be divided into three broad categories:

- physical methods
- community action
- design factors.

Physical methods include all the machinery and technology which can be used to make crime more difficult, such as alarms or surveillance systems. Community awareness can both reduce the risk of crime and increase the rate of conviction. Design, especially of buildings, can be used to persuade potential criminals that committing an offence in a particular environment is simply too risky.

About 95% of crime is committed against property rather than against the person. Most violent crimes occur after 11 o'clock at night when alcohol is often a factor. This means that, for managers of leisure and tourism companies, theft and fraud are the offences they will most likely have to deal with. Hotels and leisure centres must do all they can to make breaking into rooms or lockers and theft of luggage or handbags difficult.

Many tourism operations, for example attractions, are cash businesses. They face the same risk of robberies as banks, building societies and shops. They can make use of some of the technology developed to make robbery more difficult. Areas where counter staff work with the public, such as a currency exchange centre, can have rapid rising screens fitted. In less than a second these will place an opaque barrier between the would-be robber and the counter staff. Time lapse safes also have the effect of delaying the robber, few of whom will want to take the chance of waiting around for an hour or two until the safe can be opened again! These can be set for a shorter time lapse, so that customers genuinely wishing to withdraw or exchange cash can be asked to return in 10 or 15 minutes.

Premises wishing to create a friendly, informal atmosphere may be reluctant to put up too many barriers between customers and staff. They can, however, still use electronic devices such as metal detectors installed in the entrance. These will indicate if anyone is carrying any larger than usual metal objects.

The physical movement of money from business premises to security vans represents a vulnerable point in protecting the cash. There are two technological developments which help in detecting this type of crime:

● a smoke and dye system will release smoke from cash bags, leaving a dye on the money and those handling it
● security vehicles can be fitted with surveillance systems which enable a monitor at a base station to pick up a signal from the vehicle. This means that its movements can be tracked accurately and any departure from the agreed route immediately passed on to the police.

Other technological advances have been employed in the fight against crime. In 1990 some £2 billion was spent by industry as a whole on security equipment. This included closed circuit television surveillance, electronic access control systems, electronic article surveillance (more commonly known as **tagging**), and alarm systems.

The access control systems are often used in hotels: swipe cards can be used to give limited or full access to hotel rooms to different staff, depending on whether their particular responsibilities require them to use specific rooms or areas.

Tagging can make the theft of valuable retail items more difficult by triggering an alarm if the goods are taken out of the shop. Some premises in the leisure industry house priceless items, like famous works of art. These can be protected by a curtain of invisible infra-red beams which, if penetrated, will set off an alarm.

More sophisticated electronic equipment may be inappropriate, and too costly, for the many smaller operations which are part of the leisure and tourism industry. A small guest house, for example, will probably have to rely on more basic security. They will need to ensure that room keys are not left hanging in public places while guests are out. Locks should conform to British Standard 3621 which would lessen the chances of them being opened by a random selection of keys. Ground floor windows can be given some protection by planting dense, prickly shrubs beneath them, though these may make cleaning more difficult! Where the premises have a car park, the owners should try to ensure that cars are as visible as possible. They are also advised to put up signs advising visitors both to lock their cars and to remove any valuables from them.

Co-operation within local business communities can be valuable. Business watch schemes encourage property-marking so that the origin of stolen goods can be traced. Action against suspected theft is often not possible simply because property cannot be accurately identified. Reporting suspicious circumstances can reveal local criminal patterns and help to combat them. Conducting a regular **crime audit** can help to establish whether resources and materials are going missing, and more importantly, from where.

Some leisure and tourism companies also face a threat from terrorism. This may be a long-term threat based on the geographical location of the building or the nature of the business itself. Premises next to military offices carry a higher risk than average. The offices of some national airlines or shops selling animal furs may also be possible targets. The fact that Madame Tussauds and the Tower at Canary Wharf have been targeted by terrorist organisations emphasises that publicity is the terrorists' aim and any company with a high public profile should be aware of the threat. Sometimes the terrorist threat may be short-term. This might be the consequence of a visit from a well known public figure or from someone with military or diplomatic connections.

Measures to counter the threat of terrorism are often a matter of common sense. The basic security of buildings needs to be thorough. Problems often occur where several companies share premises and access is not controlled. There is often no reception area and the credentials of visitors are not checked, nor are they fetched and accompanied to the office of the person they have come to see. Premises like large office blocks and hotels need a **contingency plan**, known by all occupants, so that if they need to evacuate the building they can move rapidly to a safe place.

Some simple matters of good organisation can make terrorism more difficult:

- the more tidy a working area is, the more difficult it is to conceal explosive or fire-raising devices in it
- staff should always be alert
- staff should be sure to make eye-to-eye contact with customers: potential terrorists will feel less confident that they have remained unnoticed
- personnel taking incoming telephone calls need to be trained to handle bomb threats so that they extract as much information as possible. An easy way of doing this is to use a **pro forma** which suggests the questions they should ask and what they should listen out for. Accurate information about the location and timing of the threatened bomb is needed so that the company can make a quick response. The police would obviously hope for additional information about such things as accent, background noise, and what organisation the terrorist claimed to represent.

One of the main problems in dealing with business crime, particularly fraud, is the reluctance to report it. Few managing directors would wish to admit to shareholders that their companies had been defrauded. Leisure attractions face a different problem in admitting the threat of crime. People out for a pleasurable day do not want to be constantly reminded of the threat of pickpockets or car thieves.

The three principles of physical methods, community awareness and design are likely to guide the future of crime prevention.

- New physical means will be found, such as the plan to develop an air tube system which could move small sums of money from businesses direct to banks and which could be immediately shut down if they were tampered with.
- Building good community relations will continue to be a means of exchanging ideas on ways to prevent crime and raising the levels of awareness.
- Designers will work with architects to make sure that security features are built into new business premises.

## Your tasks

I  Discuss business security in the leisure and tourism industry and what can be done to improve it. Use the following questions as the basis of your discussion:
  a)  What is a surveillance system? Where is it likely to be most effective?
  b)  In what ways do you think community awareness can reduce the frequency of crime?
  c)  What design features might persuade criminals that robbing a particular theme park was too risky?

**d)** What practical and feasible ways can you suggest of reducing the chances of luggage theft at airports?

**e)** If you had a time lapse safe in a leisure or tourism business, what factors would determine the time settings you would use?

**f)** What advice would you give to a small theatre owner about banking cash takings?

**g)** Can you suggest ways in which technology could be used to make the theft of computers and other business machines less worthwhile?

**h)** Can you list some practical things which a business watch scheme might do to reduce the risk of crime in a specific business area?

**i)** What do you think would be suitable questions for a police pro forma to be used by receptionists or telephonists answering bomb threat calls?

**j)** Do you think it should be an offence not to report a crime such as theft or fraud?

**2** Choose a specific leisure or tourism facility. Write a short report to include:

- how much security there is at present
- how vulnerable it is to crime
- what improvements you would suggest to reduce the risk.

# 2.7 Inflatable play equipment: user safety

**Develops knowledge and understanding of the following element:**

**2** Propose ways of enabling the health and safety of customers and staff

**Supports the development of the following core skills:**

Communication level 3: Prepare written material (Task 1)

*There are guidelines for the use of inflatable play equipment.*

Many tourist attractions are now aware of the influence of children in deciding where families go on excursions. This may be seen in a more active approach in museums, reduced admission and catering prices for family groups or, increasingly, through the provision of children's play equipment.

To meet the demands of one-off events and festivals a number of companies began producing inflatable play devices which could be taken down and moved much more quickly than more permanent playground equipment. These devices caused a number of safety problems, some to do with the structures themselves and others because they were usually hired by event organisers and it was not clearly stated who was responsible for carrying out safety procedure.

Injuries reported as a result of children using these inflatables include fractures, dislocations, sprains and bruising. Bouncing castles, a popular form of inflatable play device, have caused enough concern for the Health and Safety Executive to produce specific guidelines about using them. The guidelines list several possible dangers:

- the castle blowing over
- the fabric splitting under pressure from users
- overcrowding
- older children using the castle at the same time as smaller ones
- air loss
- dangerous positioning of the equipment.

### Your task

1 Write your own set of guidance notes for operators in charge of setting up and supervising bouncing castles. Issues you might cover could include:
- crowd control
- access to the inflatable
- site suitability
- anchorage
- supervision
- training of attendants
- behaviour of users
- inspection and maintenance of the castle
- design of the inflatable.

# 2.8 Activity holidays: customer safety

**Develops knowledge and understanding of the following element:**
2 Propose ways of enabling the health and safety of customers and staff

**Supports the development of the following core skills:**
Communication level 3: Prepare written material (Tasks 1, 2, 3)

The days when people spent their whole holiday asleep in a deck chair are, for many, long gone. Travel brochures now advertise tours in which people can try white water canoeing, hot air ballooning, abseiling or even driving racing cars. Tour operators who offer these activities can do a number of things to make them as safe as possible, apart from investing in very sound insurance schemes.
- The qualifications and skills of the staff they hire are vital: a non-swimming water ski instructor, for example, would be a severe liability.
- The activity centres should be required to record all accidents and provide a full explanation of how and why each one occurred.
- Supervision needs to be thorough: centres need to allow for the fact that many accidents happen at times when no formal activity or instruction is taking place, particularly where children are involved.

Two types of activity holiday which carry particular risk of injury are pony-trekking and water sports. Ponies may look sweet, biddable creatures in travel brochures, but they can be obstinate and unpredictable. Since trekking is often across rough and remote terrain, the consequences of being thrown can be very serious. The hot summers of 1990 and 1991 led to an increase of algae in many stretches of fresh water. Anyone taking part in water sports who swallowed any of this could suffer serious after-effects. In spite of this there is no legal requirement for staff at activity centres to have first aid qualifications.

The Department for Education has published a document called Safety in Outdoor Pursuits which recommends safety procedures for outdoor holiday centres. It covers points and suggestions such as the following:

● the most appropriate ratios of leaders or instructors to students on different activities
● careful inspection of the training and qualifications claimed by instructors
● high standard and regularly inspection of equipment.

Activities like skiing carry higher risks of injury than many others, not all of them due to slippery conditions under foot. The most common injuries suffered are pulled muscles and twisted joints, but there could be fewer of these if holiday-makers followed training programmes aimed at improving their fitness before they set off. Skiing falls can be caused by incompetence, but are often due to fatigue as well. Exercises like running or cycling can improve individual stamina and reduce the risk of falls resulting from tiredness.

## Your tasks

Mr Wally Tempty owns a remote hill farm in North Wales. In recent years he has found it increasingly difficult to make a decent living from farming. He applied for and gained planning permission to renovate a barn on his land and convert it to dormitory-style accommodation for 20 visitors.

The farm is 30 miles from the village of Llanmad, where shops and the local doctor can be found. The regional hospital and fire services are a further 20 miles away in Abersynglais. He proposed to lay out a dirt race track over hilly ground (see the sketch map below). His proposal was accepted largely because his farm is so remote. He has

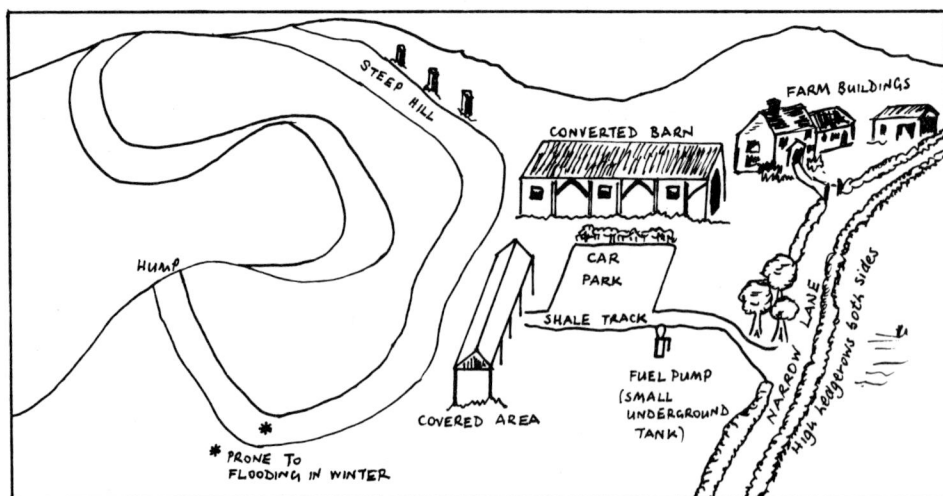

*Mr Wally Tempty's sketch map of his farm, showing his development proposals*

now completed the track and has bought six mountain bikes and six motor cycle scramblers, all second hand.

He has marketed his facilities largely to appeal to youth club and school parties.

1 List the potential hazards involved in Mr Tempty's scheme to encourage people to come and stay on his farm.

2 Draw up a series of proposals which you think would reduce the risks as far as possible. Comment on their cost and how practical they would be.

3 Write a contingency plan for Mr Tempty and any staff he employs to follow in the event of an accident or emergency.

# 2.9 Using technology to improve security

**Develops knowledge and understanding of the following elements:**
3    Propose ways of enhancing security in leisure and tourism

**Supports the development of the following core skills:**
Communication level 3: Read and respond to written material and images (Task 1)
Communication level 3: Prepare written material (Tasks 2, 3)

Theft can be a problem in any facility where visitors are likely to be separated from their belongings for any length of time. Hotel bedrooms or changing rooms in leisure facilities are particularly vulnerable areas. Generally the larger the facility, the greater the concern, since where there are more people about there are more opportunities for thieves to make themselves inconspicuous.

Recent technological developments should help to improve the security of guests and visitors in large facilities by improving locking systems and making it more difficult for thieves to open doors and lockers. With traditional keys there is always the small chance that the occupier of a room could copy or keep a key. These keys are being replaced, especially in large hotels, by systems using magnetic strip cards. The magnetic strip, like those on credit cards, carries a code. The card is used to unlock the door and the code is copied to a microprocessor in the lock itself. Once this has been done no other card, apart from a master carried by hotel personnel, will open the lock. If a card is lost, a newly coded card can be issued immediately so that the lost card will no longer open the lock.

The system carries a number of in-built advantages. Each time a new guest books into a hotel they will carry a card with a different code from the previous user of the room. The coded cards can be processed before the guest arrives. The information stored in the lock's microprocessor can be used by security staff to tell how often the door has been opened and whether the guest's card or a master card was used each time. The most recently developed systems have an option which allows guests to use their own credit cards to gain access to their rooms.

Though the main use of such cards is to provide the user with access to a room or locker, the cards could also be coded to admit the holders to lifts, night entrances, room safes or garages. This would reduce the opportunity for unauthorised people to enter.

There are benefits to the owners of the facilities as well as to the visitors from using electronic locking systems. Apart from improving their image as safe and secure places to stay, they can use the systems to collect information which may be useful for future marketing. The functions of the magnetic cards could cover additional charges from the stay, for cable television, for example, leisure facilities or business services. The spending habits of individual guests can be stored and analysed through the facility's central computing system and used as the basis for future advertising and promotions.

## Your tasks

1 Mrs Ava Roome has had her large country house converted into 12 bed and breakfast apartments, but has kept three rooms on the ground floor as her own living quarters. She is aware of concerns about theft, but also thinks that a friendly atmosphere is essential for her business to do well.

List the advantages and disadvantages of each of the following possible decisions she is considering taking:

a) providing locks and keys for all apartments, but not for her own living quarters

b) providing locks and keys for all apartments and for her own rooms

c) providing no locks inside the house at all

d) installing an electronic locking system for all rooms.

2 Write a circular letter from Mr I.D. Stringer-Mupp, the Managing Director of Safe as Houses Limited, manufacturers of a range of electronic locking systems, to be sent to hotels known to be still using key systems.

Your letter should outline the potential advantages of installing an electronic system, and should deal with points which hotel owners would be likely to ask about, for example cost, installation, training and maintenance.

3 Choose an outdoor event, such as a rock concert or an agricultural show, which is likely to attract a large number of visitors.

What do you think that the organisers and the police will feel are the main security risks?

Write a report explaining how the potential uses of technology could improve the security of the people taking part, and of their possessions.

Your report should cover:

● the availability of equipment

● the budget allowed for security

● the practical problems involved in using the technology.

# 2.10  Preventing theft in the hospitality industry

**Develops knowledge and understanding of the following element:**
3    Propose ways of enhancing security in leisure and tourism

**Supports the development of the following core skills:**
Communication level 3: Take part in discussions (Tasks 1, 2)

Some recent research suggested that as many as a quarter of the staff working in the hospitality industry are likely at some time to overcharge or cheat customers. The opportunities clearly exist, especially for employees operating in busy areas where surveillance is difficult. It is difficult to judge the extent of the problem since many such crimes go unreported. Prosecution might be a lesson to others, but hotel and bar owners often simply do not want the bad publicity it attracts.

The most common reasons given for staff theft are
- lack of regular supervision
- rapid turnover of cash
- the relatively low wages paid in many areas of hospitality.

Preventing such thefts can be approached in a number of ways.
- The **ethos** of the company and the effectiveness of the personnel department may significantly reduce or eliminate theft, especially in smaller operations.
- Using computerised tills will help, if the reports which they produce are studied carefully. If, however, employees intending to steal run reports to check that the exact amount has been removed from the till to cover the difference between what customers paid and what the till registered, they may avoid discovery. Ironically, a busy till used by honest staff for a day will almost certainly show up small discrepancies.
- Observation of staff at work is the obvious way of preventing theft. Concealed video cameras can be used, though any method of surveillance is unlikely to uncover useful evidence if the staff under suspicion are aware that they are being watched.
- Another method is to set up customers to offer the exact money for an order. If they need change, employees have to open the till, but being handed the right money gives them an opportunity either to steal or to show their honesty.
- Searching the bags, pockets and lockers of employees is carried out by some companies, though to keep good staff relations companies who do this generally make this intention clear when any new member of staff is appointed.

If an employer reports a theft to the police, they will prosecute only if they believe that there is enough evidence to have a reasonable chance of securing a conviction. Some employers think that video surveillance and a policy of prosecuting all employees found guilty of theft is the best deterrent against future stealing. Others believe that the best ways to eliminate theft are to vet potential employees carefully, looking closely at references and past employment histories, and to provide training which emphasises the importance of personal integrity.

> ### Your tasks
>
> 1 Look carefully at each of the following situations. Discuss what possible courses of action a manager might take and decide, in each case, which action you think would be the most appropriate:
>    ● a cloakroom attendant fails to issue tickets for all garments received and when challenged, claims that some regular customers have easily recognisable coats and don't want to be bothered with tickets
>    ● an employee in a restaurant bar frequently uses the 'No Sale' key on an electronic till and when asked why, says that it is a way of using the till as an adding machine for working out larger orders
>    ● a sports centre cashier records an exceptionally high number of unused facilities covering a range of sporting activities and when challenged, claims that these are the result of late cancellations
>    ● a car park attendant is reported by a member of the public for offering to resell unexpired parking tickets at a reduced rate and when asked for an explanation, claims that the offer had come from the motorist who had seen him pick up the abandoned ticket.
>
> 2 Prepare a short induction talk to be given to new employees in either:
>    ● the food service area of a large airport, or
>    ● the busy bar areas of a large tourist attraction.
>    Your talk should cover the company's views and policy on the subject of theft, the standards expected by the company and the ways in which these standards are monitored

# 2.11 Security training for staff: Thorpe Park

**Develops knowledge and understanding of the following element:**
3    Propose ways of enhancing security in leisure and tourism

**Supports the development of the following core skills:**
Communication level 3: Prepare written material (Tasks 1, 2, 3)

Thorpe Park, a leisure park near Chertsey, in Surrey, receives more than a million visits a year. The site covers 500 acres, including large stretches of water, and visitors stay on average for six hours. All new employees undergo a training programme which stresses the importance of security. Staff are described as members of a cast, putting on a daily show for the benefit of the public. The extract below from Thorpe Park's training booklet *On with the Show* describes each employee's security responsibilities.

We are all responsible for maintaining the high level of security at Thorpe Park. Immediately report any thefts, loss of or damage to the Park's property to your Supervisor and Operations Control.

Be alert to suspicious incidents or people and report them at once.

If you find or are handed any lost property, immediately check for items of value in the presence of another person. All lost property must be handed in to the Visitor Services Point at the earliest opportunity and entered in the Lost Property Register. You are personally responsible for such property until it is handed in; therefore you should not leave it in your workplace overnight or hand it to another Cast Member. If you are unable to hand in an item of lost property immediately, particularly a valuable item such as a purse or handbag, telephone the Visitor Services Point to advise them that this item has been found.

Always be aware of the security of your own property.

Cast Members are not permitted to carry any money into the Park.

Female Cast Members may take a small make-up bag to work. Apart from this, Cast Members are not permitted to carry personal bags into the Park.

Random spot searches will be carried out.

### Your security pass

Your security pass is an essential part of your costume. It enables you to:
- sign in and out for work
- obtain your costume
- obtain locker keys
- collect your till float (where applicable)
- cash a cheque at the Cast Control.

## Your tasks

1 Devise an exercise, to be used as part of the training programme for new staff at a leisure park, to make them more aware of how to identify 'suspicious incidents or people'.

2 Outline a scheme to make visitors to a popular tourist attraction more conscious of protecting their own property against theft; remember that you do not want to give the impression that the attraction is completely unsafe to visit because of the high crime risk.

3 Some leisure and tourism facilities insist that staff wear visible identification, carrying their names, and sometimes photographs.
Choose several leisure and tourism workplaces and list the possible advantages and disadvantages of such a practice in each of them.

# Unit 3  Providing customer care

## 3.1  Welcoming overseas visitors

**Develops knowledge and understanding of the following element:**
1    Identify the role of customer service in a leisure and tourism facility

**Supports the development of the following core skills:**
Application of number level 3: Interpret and present mathematical data (Tasks 1, 3)
Communication level 3: Prepare written material (Task 2)

Any country wishing to attract overseas visitors needs to be aware of the first impressions their visitors receive. If this is a long wait at Passport Control followed by an unfriendly grilling by Customs and Excise staff, the chances of a return visit have already been reduced. If customers are to feel that their needs are being successfully met, they expect to be treated with efficiency and courtesy.

Efficiency is often a matter of having sufficient staff to ensure that queues move rapidly through passport and customs controls. The advantages which the opening of the Channel Tunnel will bring will be partly lost if there are long delays for passengers crossing from one country to another. Perhaps carrying out immigration clearance procedures on board, now available with some coach passengers, will become more common.

One method of trying to ensure good customer care is to set performance standards. The Government is to introduce these at

*Travellers need to be treated with efficiency and courtesy.*

45

Gatwick and Heathrow, setting a target of three minutes as the maximum wait for any EC national entering Britain before being seen by an immigration officer. Another possible method of speeding up the process is to clear visitors at their point of embarkation. This would have to be negotiated very thoroughly with the company providing the transport, but the 1988 Immigration Act does provide for **private sector** organisations to pay for extra immigration facilities in order to get a superior service for their customers.

Customs and Excise officers have the difficult task of preventing smuggling while causing the least amount of inconvenience to innocent passengers. Most arrival points in the United Kingdom present the visitor with a choice of Red or Green Channels, depending on whether they have goods in their possession on which import taxes are due. Leaflets and posters on transport and at points of entry are intended to make people rapidly aware of their tax-free allowances. Recent attempts to speed up the process include 'Red Points' where passengers can make an early declaration of the goods they are carrying, sometimes before they collect their luggage. All passengers then go through an open spot check.

Courtesy is equally important in welcoming foreign visitors. When there are delays or people need to be questioned, visitors should always be given a clear explanation. When luggage has to be searched, customs officers should offer to help repack cases. Customs officers now wear name badges (it was felt that this would make them seem more human), and their training insists that they are courteous at all times.

## Midshire Airport

Midshire Airport is a small but developing airport which receives 72 incoming flights per day between the hours of 8 am and 9 pm. The average number of daily incoming passengers remains fairly constant at around 8000. The table below shows the number of flights and the average number of passengers arriving from within the UK, the European Community, the USA and countries outside these areas.

| Time period | from UK | from EC | from USA | from others |
|---|---|---|---|---|
| 0800–0900 | 2-220 | 0-0 | 1-130 | 0-0 |
| 0900–1000 | 5-560 | 1-120 | 2-320 | 1-200 |
| 1000–1100 | 3-280 | 3-350 | 0-0 | 0-0 |
| 1100–1200 | 3-250 | 2-310 | 0-0 | 0-0 |
| 1200–1300 | 2-190 | 2-240 | 0-0 | 1-220 |
| 1300–1400 | 1-150 | 1-120 | 0-0 | 0-0 |
| 1400–1500 | 2-200 | 0-0 | 0-0 | 0-0 |
| 1500–1600 | 3-310 | 2-180 | 0-0 | 1-200 |
| 1600–1700 | 4-360 | 2-180 | 0-0 | 0-0 |
| 1700–1800 | 5-410 | 2-190 | 0-0 | 0-0 |
| 1800–1900 | 6-500 | 2-150 | 0-0 | 1-190 |
| 1900–2000 | 3-330 | 1-140 | 1-140 | 0-0 |
| 2000–2100 | 2-180 | 1-120 | 2-300 | 2-270 |

## Your tasks

1 Study the following questions. To what extent do you think they might affect the levels of customer care provided at Midshire Airport?

a) What fluctuations in the flow of incoming passengers are evident during the day?

b) What problems are created by the management specifying that Customs and Immigration staff work in continuous 8-hour shifts?

c) Would a split-shift system mean that a better service could be offered to the public?

2 The catering services at Midshire Airport are due for a complete overhaul. Draw up a list of general recommendations showing where you think the management should concentrate their main efforts in order to meet the likely needs of incoming passengers.

You should consider issues relating to time, personnel and types of cuisine.

3 A survey of incoming passengers has revealed the following statistics:

- 20 per cent of all arrivals would prefer to travel from the airport to the city of Midtown, some 15 minutes drive away, by taxi
- 50 per cent prefer the cheaper option of the half-hourly bus service (current capacity: 60 passengers)
- 30 per cent are either met by friends or relatives or have parked their own cars in nearby suburbs, as the airport does not as yet have a long stay car park.

Assume that on average two passengers travel in each taxi, the management is considering modifying the bus service timetable, and that funds have been promised to improve the car parking facilities. Draw up a plan to respond as far as possible to the customer needs as expressed in the survey.

# 3.2 Museums and galleries: looking after the public

**Develops knowledge and understanding of the following element:**

1   Identify the role of customer service in a leisure and tourism facility

**Supports the development of the following core skills:**

Communication level 3: Take part in discussions (Task 1)
Communication level 3: Prepare written material (Task 2)
Communication level 3: Take part in discussions (Task 3)

People visiting museums and art galleries have several different hopes for their visit. Some may expect to view works of art in complete peace and quiet. They need an atmosphere which encourages reflection and contemplation. Others are hungry for information, feeling that they need the kind of background detail which a guide can provide so that they can fully experience what they are seeing. Children may find neither of these types of experience sufficiently interesting to hold their attention for long. A museum or gallery will also need to ensure the safety of often extremely valuable exhibits, so it is easy to see that an attendant may find it hard to fulfil all these needs at once.

   The role of museum and gallery attendants is not generally a very exciting one. They are often stationed in the same room all day. Although they are responsible for surveillance and

A guided tour of the Science and Industry Museum, Manchester

security, they are rarely called into action to safeguard exhibits. They are more likely either to have to ask visitors to make less noise or to direct them to other areas of the building. The combination of the tedium of the job and the fact that the public see the attendant as a sort of a policeman can mean that it is difficult to establish good relationships between visitors and attendants.

How good a service attendants provide for visitors may well depend on how the museum or gallery approaches staff development. If attendants are encouraged to acquire and pass on knowledge about the exhibits they are responsible for, this can raise their self-esteem. Training which emphasises the long-term objectives of the gallery or museum and which encourages attendants to feel part of the process of change and development can also be a positive influence. The attendants need to be made to feel that the reputation of their workplace and its capacity to attract visitors depend on their manner and enthusiasm as much as on the exhibits themselves.

Judging how to react to individual visitors is a critical part of any training programme. Well informed attendants could provide information to obviously curious visitors, but would need to realise when not to inflict lectures on those wanting peace and quiet or those just wanting a quick visit. It is also important that attendants understand the information they are passing on, as the answers they give to visitors' questions should be as accurate as possible.

## Your tasks

1 Identify a particular room in a gallery or museum which you have visited.
   Discuss with a partner the most appropriate replies which an attendant in your chosen room could give to the following:
   a) Excuse me, is this picture/exhibit very famous?
   b) Where are the toilets, mate?
   c) Is it OK to take photographs?
   d) Can't you do something about the temperature – it's far too hot – and shutting

those kids up wouldn't go amiss either...

e) Why don't you have signs up in French?

f) I've lost my mum...

g) You should be ashamed putting all this old rubbish on public display. Who's paying for it? That's what I'd like to know!

2 Outline a strategy to help the attendant in your chosen room to remain interested and enthusiastic throughout their working day.

3 Devise a series of role plays which could be used as part of a training programme for the attendant of your room. The role plays should encourage:
- an ability to communicate fluently
- the use of appropriate body language
- a polite and courteous manner
- an ability to provide background information when requested
- the use of tact and common sense
- enthusiasm for the job.

# 3.3 Customers with special needs: wheelchair access

**Develops knowledge and understanding of the following element:**

2    Plan a customer care programme

**Supports the development of the following core skills:**

Communication level 3: Read and respond to written material and images (Task 1)

Communication level 3: Prepare written material (Task 2)

The Holiday Care Service is a national charity which provides holiday information and support for disabled people, single parents, those on low incomes, carers and anyone else in need.

The Holiday Service joined with the four National Tourist Boards – in England, Wales, Scotland and Northern Ireland – in the Tourism for All campaign. One part of this campaign was the launch in 1990 of a system of identifying which types of accommodation provide access for wheelchair users and others who have difficulty walking.

The regional tourist boards put the places inspected into one of three categories. The system is applied not only to hotels and guest houses but also to self-catering apartments, camping and caravan sites and chalets. Crown, key and Q systems enable potential visitors to judge the general facilities and quality standards of accommodation they may be planning to use.

Inspected premises which reach the standards suggested by the Holiday Care Service may display an 'Accessible' symbol which will indicate the category they have been awarded.

- To achieve category 3 they must be accessible to a wheelchair user who is also able to walk a short distance and up at least three steps.

**49**

- Category 2 means the accommodation is also accessible to a wheelchair user with assistance.
- Category 1 means that the accommodation is accessible to a wheelchair user travelling alone.

The criteria used could have been stricter, but it was argued that this would have reduced the choice of places to stay to the very small number designed or adapted for easy and regular wheelchair use.

The criteria which have to be met before the 'Accessible' symbol can be displayed cover a number of areas.

- A public entrance must be accessible from a car park or setting down point.
- If the accommodation has a car park, a reservable space should be made available when required. This space should have a minimum width of 3.6 metres for Category 1.
- The route from the car park to the entrance should be free of obstacles, with no more than three steps for Category 3, and one step for Category 2.
- A level or ramped path must be available to qualify for Category 1.

There are a number of conditions laid down for the inside of all types of inspected accommodation.

- At least one bedroom and, where they are present, one lounge and one restaurant or dining room must be accessible to a wheelchair user.
- The top two categories (1 and 2) must have an accessible restaurant table with adequate space underneath for a wheelchair user to eat in comfort.
- There are minimum measurements for doorways, spaces beyond doors and corridors.
- The number of steps permissible within each category is the same inside the building as outside.
- Lifts must be large enough to hold a wheelchair, and for Category 1 automatic doors and controls must be within reach.
- Bedrooms and bathrooms require a number of specific conditions before they are approved by inspectors.
- There must be sufficient bedside space for a wheelchair user to transfer from wheelchair to bed and vice versa.
- Controls for television, lights, other switches and door handles and locks must be within reach.
- Bathrooms and toilets require good access and adequate space for manoeuvre.
- Suitable support rails are essential if any accommodation is to be placed in Category 1 or 2.

### Your tasks

I Answer the following questions based on information given in the passage:
   a) Why do you think the Tourism for All campaign was launched?
   b) What difficulties might individual providers of tourist accommodation have if they wish to adapt their premises for wheelchair users?
   c) Can you name any activities within holiday accommodation, but not mentioned in the passage, which wheelchair visitors might find easier if there is some special provision?

**d)** A large hotel is thinking of employing a wheelchair user. How do you think this might affect the hotel?

2 The 'Accessible' scheme is being extended so that it will cover fully self-catering accommodation and holiday caravan and camping parks.
Draw up a detailed list of criteria which could be used to award the three 'Accessible' symbols in each of the two following accommodation areas:
- the kitchens of self-catering apartments
- the layout of a camping and caravan site.

# 3.4 Customer care: staff appearance

**Develops knowledge and understanding of the following element:**
2    Plan a customer care programme

**Supports the development of the following core skill:**
Communication level 3: Take part in discussions (Tasks 1, 2)

New leisure and tourism facilities have to decide how customers will be able to recognise company employees. First impressions are important, and the appearance of both staff coming into contact with customers and the facility itself will determine whether visitors leave with a positive impression.

If customers have doubts about the appearance of company employees, even if these are based on personal dislikes, it will be more difficult to win their trust – essential if the company is in the business of selling to them. Customers are, of course, individuals but many companies take the view that the majority may still dislike, for example, men wearing earrings or women in trousers and they may discourage these among their staff.

Uniforms have a number of potential advantages.
- They help customers to identify staff easily.
- They can be a means of marketing: the styles and colours can match the company logo and be emphasised in advertising and promotion.
- If the design and materials are well chosen, a uniform can help boost morale and help to retain staff.

As most people will remember from schooldays, however, wearing a uniform does not automatically make people look smart, and telling someone else how they should look without giving offence requires

*A member of staff at a theme park in entertainment costume*

**51**

sensitivity. Companies such as airlines, where a high standard of smartness is demanded, may give cabin staff very specific guidance about what make-up, hair styles and jewellery are acceptable. Similarly cleanliness is a sensitive but vital area for any company whose employees are in regular contact with customers: few of us wish to be served by someone who is dirty or smelly.

The appearance of the facility itself – whether it is a travel agency, a hotel room, or an attraction – is equally important. For example, if a travel agent's window contains only untidy handwritten lists of holiday offers, potential customers will go elsewhere. If it is dimly lit and the brochures are organised in such a way that it is difficult for people to find what they want, customers will not stay long. There may be very little floor space but half-empty coffee cups and ash trays full of old cigarette ends can easily be kept away from public areas. People often browse through brochures in a travel agency without returning them neatly to the proper rack. Attention to this and small details such as keeping the special offers advertised up-to-date can go a long way towards giving customers a good first impression.

## Your tasks

1  Write a brief description of the different uniforms worn by three individuals you have seen working in leisure and tourism.
    a)  How suitable were the outfits for the jobs they were doing?
    b)  What impression did the clothes give you?
    c)  Do you think the impact on you was what was intended?
    d)  Are there any ways in which the uniform might not always create the effect the company intends?

2  The following people are key employees in new leisure and tourism ventures:
    • a woman carrying small posies of real and dried flowers in a basket to sell to tourists and theatre-goers in a city centre
    • a man, representing the British Tourist Authority at a series of trade fairs and exhibitions in Eastern Europe, with the job of encouraging people to visit Britain
    • the driver of a miniature railway which is to be installed at a model village attraction, where it will run around the perimeter
    • a woman who is to act as guide at a country house newly open to the public which contains a famous art collection and also a maze of secret passages
    • a female employee in a small new travel agency intending to specialise in tours of India and Pakistan.
    a)  What impressions do you think the employers of each of these five people would wish them to make on customers?
    b)  You are asked to design a uniform for each employee. In each case in which order would you place these three priorities:
        • durability
        • cost
        • appearance?
    c)  Suggest reasons in each case why some materials and colours would be more suitable than others.

# 3.5 Customer care: price and quality

**Develops knowledge and understanding of the following element:**

2    Plan a customer care programme

**Supports the development of the following core skills:**
Communication level 3: Read and respond to written material and images (Task 1)
Communication level 3: Take part in discussions (Tasks 2, 3)

Leisure and tourism customers are not always buying a manufactured article, but they will still want value for money. More is expected from a holiday costing £1000 than from one costing half that sum. Golfers joining a club with exceptionally high fees expect the course to be in good condition and the clubhouse to be reasonably comfortable.

Price is a very easy way of measuring competing tourism and leisure services. Tour operators in particular have used price-cutting as an important way of attracting a larger share of the market. This both drastically reduced profit margins and allowed little leeway to protect the quality of the holidays they were offering. Some companies were forced out of business as a result. Another result was that many companies' holiday packages became difficult to distinguish from those offered by their competitors.

Customers are clearly not going to pay extra for a holiday which is identical to a less expensive one. They may, however, be reluctant to buy something which they see as cheap. Customers will feel this way if they think that the low price is a result of cheap materials, poor workmanship or inferior service and facilities. Tour operators also found that by concentrating on price they tended to move down-market. This meant that they had to attract a higher number of relatively low-spending customers to make a profit. Tour operators looking for a more reliable market concentrated on quality and charged a more realistic price, so that they had fewer customers but these paid more than people going on very cheap holidays. These companies reasoned that in difficult economic times the low-spending mass market is the first to disappear.

If companies want customers to believe that price is not the only important factor, their competing products have to have distinctive qualities. In the case of holidays this might be the actual destination choice or, if customers are booking a hotel, it might be the specific leisure facilities it has to offer. Products actually made in Britain are always going to find it difficult to compete on price terms alone with similar products made in parts of the world where labour costs are very much lower.

If the customer is going to receive value for money, it is vital that the seller is fully aware of the customer's needs. A travel agent may know that its customers want a holiday, but they must find out what the customer's own preferences and previous experience are if they are to provide value for money. Even with leisure and tourism the product needs to be properly designed. For example, customers renting a badminton court in a sports hall where the next court is being used for trampolining may feel this is poor planning.

Sellers should also aiming for reliability, notoriously difficult in areas like travel where delays can be caused by events beyond the control of travel agents and tour operators themselves. Feedback from satisfied customers is critical if the reliability of something like individual holiday packages is to be established. As there is no manufactured product involved, this is the best way of gathering evidence for customers of the performance of what they are thinking of buying. A growing number of tour operators have improved the compensation they offer customers if their itineraries are disrupted. The European Community Travel Directive, launched on January 1st 1993, strengthens the **liability** of any company offering a tour package. Any company offering two elements from transport, accommodation, or other tourism services is made liable for any customer claims which arise from an accident, fatality or major disturbance affecting their booked package.

Maintaining a consistent service is essential if a company claims to offer value for money. A tour operator needs to be sure that a hotel can maintain its standards, regardless of any changes in staff or increases in occupancy rate. Forward planning is essential, particularly where maintenance or refurbishment is likely to disrupt normal business. Ideally such work should be done out of season, but operators in any case should inform customers of any unavoidable disruption.

## Your tasks

The itineraries of three tours of India are given below and on the opposite page. They are priced as follows:

- The Magic of India, from £745
- Images of India, from £1213
- The Rajah, from £933.

**1** What are the distinctive features of each of the tours on offer?

**2** Discuss the various ways in which you might try to establish which tour represented the best value for money.

**3** Working in pairs, adopt in turn the roles of travel agency counter staff and potential customer interested in touring India. You should offer the advice most appropriate to the customer's need.

# THE MAGIC OF INDIA  Escorted from Delhi back to Delhi

## 10 DAY TOUR

### ITINERARY

**1st Day** Assemble at Heathrow for the British Airways flight to Delhi.

**2nd day** Early morning arrival in Delhi where your tour escort will meet you and take you to the Oberoi Maidens Hotel. The morning is free (to catch up on sleep or relax by the swimming pool). In the afternoon visit New Delhi, with its spacious wide roads and Lutyens-designed seat of government, originally built for the British Raj.

**3rd day** Morning tour of Old Delhi, the 17th century city called Shahjahanabad still reminiscent of Mogul times with its maze of alleys and bazaars dominated by the magnificent Red Fort and the marble domed Jama Masjid mosque. Afternoon free.

**4th day** Full morning's journey by road to Agra calling en route at Sikandra, burial place of Akbar the Great. Stay at the Clarks Shiraz Hotel. In the evening

there may be an opportunity to visit the incomparable and romantic Taj Mahal by moonlight.

**5th day** Morning visit to the Mogul Red Fort and to the Taj Mahal by daylight, still beautiful but not so mysterious. Afternoon at leisure.

**6th day** We have a day travelling to Jaipur but calling en route at Fatehpur Sikri built by Akbar in AD 1575 and deserted after a few years though the magnificent Mogul buildings still remain intact. Travel on to Bharatpur, previously a royal hunting reserve but now a bird sanctuary. (This reserve will not be included from April to June.) In the afternoon continue to Jaipur and the Clarks Amer Hotel.

**7th day** In the morning we have a tour of this rose-red city visiting the Hawa Mahal (Palace of the Winds) and the Maharajah's Palace. Afternoon free.

**8th day** Visit Amber, The old city of

Jaipur, and take an elephant ride to the Palace set on a hill dominating the town. We return to the Oberoi Maidens Hotel, Delhi in the afternoon.

**9th day** At leisure. Alternatively leave Delhi for one of our extension holidays.

**10th day** Early morning departure by British Airways for London, where we arrive at 1.00 p.m.

Meals: continental breakfast and dinner each day.

### HOTELS

The hotels chosen for the Magic of India tour have been carefully selected and represent excellent value for money. All properties have full facilities., including pool and pleasant gardens, and are of medium standard. India is a thrilling experience, but the first-time visitor should allow differences in standards to those in Europe.

# Images of India

9-night holiday – price includes Intercontinental flights on British Airways or Air India • Accommodation with private bathroom • Return airport to hotel transfers • Sightseeing as detailed • Services of Tour Escorts Days 2 to 10 • Jetset Luxury Travel Kit

*India – a country of diverse cultures, architectures, peoples, landscapes history, sights, sounds and mysteries. This tour offers a superb introduction, encompassing some of India's most fascinating and awe-inspiring attractions. Marvel at the splendour of Delhi's Red Fort, and at the intricate facade of Jaipur's fabled Palace of the Winds. Experience the spell-binding beauty of Agra's Taj Mahal, the famous erotic carvings at Khajuraho, and the intriguing city of Varanasi on the sacred waters of the Ganges. You also have the option of visiting Kathmandu in Nepal, in the foothills of the Himalayas, or the scenic lakeland of Srinagar in Kashmir.*

**ITINERARY**
**Departs – Sun**
Hotel nights – Delhi 2, Jaipur 2, Agra 1, Khajuraho 1, Varanasi 1, Delhi 1.

**Day 1 London/Delhi**
Depart London Heathrow on British Airways or Air India.

**Day 2 Delhi**
Arrive in Delhi early this morning and transfer to the Taj Mahal hotel. Today is free to explore.

**Day 3 Delhi**
Morning at leisure. Your afternoon sightseeing tour of Old and New Delhi includes the Qurab Minar, Lakshminarayan Temple, Parliament House, the famous Red Fort and the beautiful Jama Masjid mosque.

**Day 4 Delhi/Jaipur**
This morning we drive to Jaipur. Visit the ancient hillside capital of Amber en route (which you approach on elephant back). Stay at the Rambagh Palace Hotel in Jaipur. Afternoon at leisure.

**Day 5 Jaipur**
Today you take a sightseeing tour of this magnificent pink city: visit the Maharaja's City Palace and its famous observatory, Jantar Mantar, and the Ram Niwas Gardens. Admire the Hawa Mahal, or Palace of the Winds, the fantastic soaring facade of pink stone.

**Day 6 Jaipur/Agra**
Depart for Agra, visiting the graceful red sandstone city of Fatehpur Sikri en route. On arrival in Agra transfer to the Taj View hotel. Afternoon at leisure.

**Day 7 Agra**
This morning visit the stunning Taj Mahal, built by the Moghul Emperor Shahjahan as a tomb for his queen. Later visit the Agra Fort with its many beautiful buildings, including the Pearl Mosque.

**Day 8 Agra/Khajuraho**
This afternoon fly to Khajuraho and the Chandela Hotel. Spend the rest of the day exploring Khajuraho.

**Day 9 Khajuraho/Varanasi**
In the morning visit the Khajuraho Temples, built by the Chandela Kings between AD 950 and 1050 and decorated with lavishly erotic Hindu sculptures. This afternoon fly to Varanasi; stay at the Taj Ganges.

**Day 10 Varanasi/Delhi**
An early morning drive through the city takes you to the riverbank for a boat ride on the holy river Ganges. See the bathing ghats, the pilgrims purifying themselves and the cremation sites. Then tour the many magnificent temples and palaces of Benaras city. In the evening fly back to Delhi where you stay at the Taj Mahal hotel.

**Day 11 Delhi/London**
Your early morning flight arrives in London around midday.

**Meals** – breakfast and dinner daily.

**Local guide escort Days 2 to 10.**

# *The Rajah*

- **Delhi**
- **Agra & Taj Mahal**
- **Jaipur**

*This short tour of the fascinating cities of Delhi, Agra and Jaipur, known as India's Golden Triangle, will show you the most popular sights of India, at a very attractive price. The hotels use are smaller and simpler than those featured on our more expensive arrangements, yet they offer a good standard of comfort and service, representing tremendous value for the budget conscious. We also offer a choice of extensions to Kashmir, Nepal, Goa or Thailand.*

**Day 1 Fri London/Delhi**
Depart Heathrow this evening by Air India flight to Delhi.

**Day 2 Sat Delhi**
On arrival in Delhi this morning, transfer to the Siddarth Hotel. The rest of the day is at leisure.

**Day 3 Sun Delhi**
During your time in Delhi, you are free to make your own discoveries in this imposing city. Perhaps take a tour of New Delhi, a city of wide avenues and imperial buildings, built by the British as the new capital of India early this century. Take a taxi to Janpath market and Connaught Place for the best shopping in Delhi or visit some of the many fascinating museums and beautiful parks which the city has to offer. Then visit Old Delhi, the city made rich and powerful by the Moghul emperors, including the huge Jama Masjid Mosque and Shah Jehan's magnificent Red Fort, Lal Qila, with its gardens, courtyards, palaces and halls. Or visit Chandni Chowk, meaning literally moonlit crossroads, and now probably the busiest street on earth. This evening why not see the Red Fort son et lumiere for a fascinating account of India's history, or a performance of Indian dances.

**Day 4 Mon Delhi/Agra**
Depart late this morning by air for Agra, for 2 nights at the Clarks Shiraz. Rest of the day at leisure. A late afternoon introductory visit to the Taj Mahal – the highlight of your trip – is recommended.

**Day 5 Tue Agra**
Day at leisure. This morning you are free to make a more leisurely tour of the Taj Mahal, India's most famous structure and often considered the world's most beautiful monument. Also try to see Itmad-ud-Daulah's smaller yet intricately decorated tomb and Agra Fort with its towering walls, marble mosques and palaces

**Day 6 Wed Agra/Jaipur**
Depart this morning by road for Jaipur. Transportation will be air conditioned on all departures between March and October. En route you will visit the deserted Moghul city of Fatehpur Sikri, built by Akbar in 1569. Arrive at your hotel, the Clarks Amer, in the afternoon, and the rest of the day is at leisure. Why not take an afternoon sightseeing tour of the beautiful walled 18th century city of Jaipur, visiting the Maharajah's Palace, Jantar Mantar – the 17th century observatory, the Central Museum of the Albert Hall and Ram Nivas Gardens.

**Day 7 Thu Jaipur**
A further day at leisure. We suggest an optional morning drive to see the delicately carved Palace of the Winds, then on to Amber, once capital of the Rajput Empire, to ride regally to the hilltop fortress on an elephant's back. At Amber Fort, see the Sheesh Mahal, (Hall of Mirrors) and the Jai Mandir (Hall of Victory). You can visit the white marble Sila Devi Temple with its clanging bells and drums. Spend the afternoon either relaxing at your hotel or exploring the city further, perhaps visiting its colourful bazaars and markets – Jaipur is well known for its gem cutting, brassware and Rajasthani cotton printing.

**Day 8 Fri Jaipur/Delhi**
About midday fly to Delhi and the Siddarth Hotel, before your transfer to the airport later tonight.

**Day 9 Sat Delhi/London**
A very early morning Air India flight to Heathrow, arriving this morning.

**Note:** It may sometimes be necessary to use hotels other than those stated.

# 3.6 Customer care techniques

**Develops knowledge and understanding of the following element:**

**3**    Provide customer service

**Supports the development of the following core skills:**

Communication level 3: Read and respond to written material and images (Task 1)

Communication level 3: Prepare written material (Task 2)

As its name suggests, customer care is about looking after customers and making sure that they feel they have benefited from contact with company employees. The leisure and tourism industry, as a service industry, is highly dependent on successful customer care. Customers often have high expectations of pleasure from holiday and leisure activity and will naturally resent any employee who appears not to be living up to these expectations.

Providing good customer care is often a matter of communication. This can only happen if the customer regards the employee as approachable in the first place. A smart appearance, an observant outlook and being willing to take the initiative in asking if help is needed can all make the customer feel more at ease.

Even when contact has been made, the customer will gain little benefit if the employee is poorly informed. An employee in a travel agency will need to have a wide knowledge of holiday destinations, but customers may also want to know about insurance details, special travel arrangements, fare supplements or luggage allowances.

Contact between customers and employees, as between any strangers, can be affected by several factors. The employee has to judge quickly what the customer's needs are and has to be a good listener to do this effectively. He or she may have to prompt the customer with questions, while at the same time trying to make sure that they don't interrupt. There may be alternative solutions and customers are entitled to know what the choices are. Providing extra information in the form of leaflets, maps, addresses or brochures often helps to meet customer needs.

*Telephone sales staff at work*

If the situation is complex, making notes may help. It can also be reassuring to both parties if the employee summarises what has been agreed at the end of the conversation. There are bound to be circumstances where an employee does not know all the answers. Rather than making up something, it is always better either to refer customers directly to someone who will know or to offer to provide information at a later time.

Not all customer contact is face to face. In leisure and tourism enquiries and reservations are often made by telephone. This often has the advantage of convenience, but it means the customer is less able get an immediate feeling for the employee's manner and personality. This makes it essential for the employee to identify themselves at the beginning of the conversation.

Businesses which are highly dependent on telephone sales may wish to keep calls within a reasonable time limit. In sales or reservations departments they may encourage the use of standard forms prompting the employee to ask a number of structured questions. In a company selling business travel this ensures that all essential information for making a reservation is given. Good customer care, however, means that the employee could depart from this 'script' if the customer wished to add an extra question. The employee would also need to be surrounded by sufficient sources of reference to be able to answer it.

Whatever the type of communication, politeness is always preferable to indifference or rudeness. Leaving customers waiting on the end of a telephone line without explaining the reason for the delay will cause irritation. Failing to acknowledge the presence of other customers while you talk at length to a customer or other member of staff will have a similar effect. Telling people, without apology, that there is nothing that can be done about their enquiry or concern is also unlikely to encourage them to return.

There may be occasions when employees are faced with giving customers some unpleasant information. They may not be entitled to a refund, their accommodation may have been changed or the time of their flight may have been delayed. Generally it is advisable to be honest about the causes of the problem. It may be necessary to explain company policy on the issue and to show the reasons for this policy rather than, for example, simply telling them that they have totally misread the small print in a brochure!

## Your tasks

1  Read the following opening remarks made in response to enquiries or questions from customers. How effective do you think they are?
   a)  I'm afraid we've made a right mess of this booking, sir...
   b)  I think it's somewhere near the town centre...
   c)  You can't really expect us to pay compensation for flight delays – that's the airline's responsibility...
   d)  I'm very sorry, madam, but as you can see we're exceptionally busy this evening. I'll certainly do everything I can to speed up the arrival of your next course...
   e)  Sorry, can you say all that again...?
   f)  Mrs Hyde's just popped out of the office. Perhaps you could ring later?

2  Write a brief guide to be used by employees operating a telephone information service in a local leisure centre.

# 3.7 Dealing with customer complaints

**Develops knowledge and understanding of the following element:**

**3**    Provide customer service

**Supports the development of the following core skills:**

Communication level 3: Take part in discussions (Task 1)

Communication level 3: Prepare written material (Task 2)

'The customer is always right' is an expression still commonly heard in service and other industries. Although an individual shop assistant or booking clerk may not always feel sympathetic to this view, there are a number of reasons why companies are increasingly concerned that customer complaints are handled with tact and diplomacy.

Customers are essential for the survival of any business and dissatisfied customers tend to go elsewhere. If their complaints are resolved successfully, they are more likely to feel that their needs and rights have been respected. The companies may also benefit by increasing the number of customers who use them again and by improving the quality of the services they offer. Additionally the company may actually enhance its reputation as a result of demonstrating that it can respond quickly and sensitively to customers' difficulties. Individual employees can gain greater job satisfaction if they are able to satisfy customers that things they have complained about will be put right.

The attitude of staff towards individual complaints is sometimes based on the assumption that these have little overall impact. Many dissatisfied customers do not voice their particular grievances, perhaps wishing to avoid confrontation. They are unlikely to return! Others will vent their frustration by telling all their friends and acquaintances, all of whom may be actual or potential customers of the same organisation. It could be argued that such customers can easily be replaced but, once marketing costs are taken into account, it is more expensive to attract new customers than to retain existing ones. Clearly there are some complainants who are out to be difficult, but research suggests that the majority simply want a reasonable response to their complaints and an improved service for themselves and others. They may actually feel that their complaint is for the good of the company. Complaining does, after all, take time and effort and often involves cost.

People will complain about a whole variety of things. In leisure and tourism complaints could include:

- the lack of a promised view from a hotel balcony
- a delayed flight
- increased charges on badminton court hire
- poor quality restaurant food.

Many complaints concern people who are supposedly working for the good of their customers. Rudeness or indifference offends people, particularly when they are seeking advice or information. When customers who already have a genuine complaint are met with rudeness or indifference, it is likely to provoke confrontation. This is particularly harmful to a company's image if it happens in a public place.

The best immediate response to most complaints is an offer of help. Establishing some kind of rapport can be useful. Many companies suggest ways of developing a genuinely sympathetic manner. Most would say it is important to 'own the problem' and not attempt to pass the blame onto someone else. Certainly employees should explain who they are and then establish the details of the complaint. Writing these down both allows the employee to clarify the facts and also gives them time to think about their response. It also suggests that the employee is interested in the problem and wishes to know what the customer would like to see done about it.

If genuine help is to be given, employees need to be fully aware of company policy. It is no use offering a compensatory free holiday to a complainant if the company then refuses to pay for it. Staff who deal with complaints do need to show that they are capable of some positive remedial action, whether it is offering a refund, a future credit or a replacement product. False promises, blaming others or putting off customers in the hope that they will lose interest in complaining may bring temporary relief but will all probably lose the company business in the long run. Many companies now have quality systems which guarantee that they will respond to complaints within a set time. Individual departments may receive pay bonuses or other incentives for meeting these targets consistently.

## Your tasks

1 Working with a partner, take alternate roles of complainant and employee in the following situations:
   - a returning holidaymaker complaining to a travel agent that the sandy beach, as described in the brochure from which the holiday was booked, was in fact shingle
   - the user of a sports hall badminton court complaining to the receptionist that it was impossible to play with a trampoline in use in an adjacent area
   - an airline passenger complaining to a member of the cabin staff about the noise made by a small child sitting with its parents in the row opposite.

   Discuss what you think would be the best approach for the company employee to take in each case.

2 Choose a specific leisure and tourism context and write a series of guidance notes to help employees in that context deal with angry customers.

# 3.8 Customer relations: the importance of body language

**Develops knowledge and understanding of the following element:**

3   Provide customer service

**Supports the development of the following core skill:**
Communication level 3: Take part in discussions (Tasks 1, 2, 3)

The impression which we give to others and the messages we pass on do not only come from the actual words which we speak. The speed at which we speak and the tone of voice we use can radically alter the impression we make. Yet a very large proportion of the message we receive from other people, and this is particularly true for people meeting for the first time, comes from the combination of gestures, postures and movements which are commonly called body language.

Many leisure and tourism employees have to be aware that, if their body language does not match what they are saying, apparently polite statements may be variously interpreted as irritation, rudeness or indifference. Since many aspects of body language are unconscious, it may require careful training to break the habit of actions which may give an unfavourable impression. Many people, for example, touch their nose or mouth when they are uncertain about something; others clench their fists or grind their teeth when they are annoyed. Lowered shoulders may mean someone is feeling relaxed; if the pupils of their eyes are contracted they may be tired or bored. Leaning forwards may suggest that someone is trying to establish dominance; leaning back may suggest defensiveness or reticence.

Being aware of body language helps to establish good relationships with customers at the outset, although it is a mistake to analyse it in isolation from what is actually said. Some common gestures and postures may have more than one possible explanation. Leaning forwards can suggest an attempt at dominance but it could also be the posture of someone with impaired hearing.

Interpreting the signals which other people give is further complicated by the fact that different nationalities and cultures may show quite distinctive body language. Staff working with tourists from overseas may appear unfriendly, confused and even give offence if they are not aware of some of these differences. In some parts of India, for example, people nod when they mean 'no'. In some countries people shake hands when they meet; in others they kiss on the cheeks. Some cultures expect young women to lower their eyes when talking to a man, while in other parts of the world that would be interpreted as a sign of unreliability.

As staff are becoming conscious of customers' body language, the process is also taking place in reverse: the customers will judge some elements of the service they receive on the tone of voice, gestures, posture and movement of the service provider. Body language may lead them to form opinions about:

- whether or not the employee likes their job
- whether they are calm or harassed
- whether they are friendly
- whether or not they respect customers
- perhaps most important of all, whether they are genuinely willing to provide help.

## Your tasks

Divide into groups of three. In each of the following three role play exercises, each person should take the role of employee in one exercise, customer in another and observer in the third.

The employee and the customer act out the scenario. (You may find it helpful to agree more specific detail for each of the scenarios before you begin.)

The observer should watch and make a note of the body language in both performances. Make notes under the following headings:

- voice
- facial expressions

- gestures
- postures
- other movements.

**1** The employee serves a customer who wishes to change travellers' cheques for currency. Passport details are requested and provided and the employee then explains the details of the exchange rate and the commission charged.

**2** A customer wishes to book a place on an aerobics course. As there are Beginners, Standard and Advanced classes, the employee has to establish the previous fitness activity of the customer. The employee then has to advise the customer that the first two sessions of the most appropriate course are fully booked.

**3** A customer visiting a museum asks an employee, who is acting as a guide, about the origins of a particular exhibit. The employee gives the official version, after which the customer offers a conflicting explanation which he or she has heard elsewhere.

# 3.9 Constructing customer questionnaires

**Develops knowledge and understanding of the following element:**
**4**     Evaluate the operation of a customer care programme.

**Supports the development of the following core skill:**
Application of number level 3: Interpret and present mathematical data (Tasks 1, 2)

Imagine that you have taken your family out for the day to a museum. There has been plenty to see, a lot of excitement and activity for the children and a great deal of walking. You are on your way out when a member of the museum staff presents you with a questionnaire with over twenty detailed answers to fill in. It is not surprising that many such questionnaires finish up in the wastepaper bin outside the main exit!

Overcoming people's reluctance is the first problem faced by the designer of a visitor questionnaire. Even where the questions are well thought out, if the visitors feel that the task is an unnecessary burden, the answers may not give a fair reflection of their attitudes. Visitors may be asked to fill in the forms at home and put them in the post, but this tends to reduce the percentage which are actually completed and returned.

The request to provide information has to be politely phrased, with a brief explanation about why the information is needed. The Museum of East Anglian Life, for example, heads its customer questionnaire with the following words:

> Before you leave the museum today, we would be most grateful if you would take the time to fill in this short questionnaire. We need to know what our visitors think so that we can continue to develop and improve the Museum and the facilities provided.

The time it takes respondents to complete the questionnaire will also affect the numbers who take the trouble to do so. The questions asked can be structured so that many of the answers only require a box to be ticked. Long or complicated questions should be avoided. Sometimes more descriptive answers may be necessary, particularly if the museum would like a range of suggestions. For example, a museum might want to ask visitors whether they had any suggestions for improvements which could be made to the facilities or services.

The actual content of the questions depends on what the devisers of the questionnaire think they need to know. They may think it is important to establish where their visitors come from. If they ask 'Where do you live?', they will collect a list of names of towns and villages which they will then have to categorise before the information tells them anything useful. If the question is phrased so that respondents have to choose from a range of options which list towns or regions, less analysis will be necessary.

Some questions will have an obvious marketing purpose. Finding out where the majority of visitors are staying will provide information about the best places to distribute publicity leaflets. Questions about who was in the visiting group, or about where they first heard of the place they are visiting will also generate data useful to the marketing department.

If the museum wants information to help to improve customer care the type of question required needs judgement and evaluation from the respondent. Care has to be taken with the wording of such questions, since it is very easy to phrase them suggesting a positive (Was the length of the queues acceptable?) or negative view ('Did you find the queues a nuisance?').

There are a number of ways in which customers can be asked to evaluate what they have seen and done.

- They can be asked to identify the best and worst: this enables a quick answer but allows for no explanation and may only draw responses about a limited number of features.
- Customers can be asked to rank features or exhibits in order of preference: this does not require much writing, but is not a very precise kind of evaluation, particularly if the list of features is long.
- The most common practice is to ask respondents to rate features on a five-point scale: very good, good, average, poor or very poor. This is still far from exact, but it does generate a general view about individual features without taking too much time to complete or analyse.

Some elements of customer care may be considered sufficiently important to have specific attention drawn to them:
- directional signs
- guides and information services
- facilities for children, the disabled or non-English speakers.

Finally, the deviser of the questionnaire tends to control what the customer is able to say, and the scope of the questions may give the respondent no chance of recording an important opinion, either constructive or critical. So most visitor surveys will end with an open invitation to comment or suggest improvements. Although these responses may be difficult to analyse, comments in response to this type of question are often the most useful in producing ideas for improving future customer care.

**Your tasks**

1 Analyse the feedback data gathered from visitor questionnaires at the Elthorne-on-Sea Toy and Games Museum.

**Elthorne-on-Sea Toy and Games Museum: summary of selected responses to visitor questionnaires**

562 responses were received, though not all respondents answered all questions.

**Question 3** — **Are you staying away from where you live?**
Yes: 415      No: 147

**Question 4(a)** — **If you are, are you staying in:**
Elthorne-on-Sea: 334    Hanstone: 31
Much Ferndon: 19    Lesser Ferndon: 4
others: 27

**Question 4(b)** — **Is your accommodation:**
Hotel: 67    Guest house: 114
Camping: 130    Self-catering: 66
Staying with friends: 38

**Question 8** — **Where did you first hear about the museum?**
Tourist information centre: 98    Leaflet: 137
Newspaper adverts: 191    Local radio: 18
Signposts: 31    From friends/locals: 87

**Question 11(a)** — **Which exhibit interested you most?**
The top 3 were:
Lady Hanstone's Dolls' House: 144    The World of Victorian Board Games: 67
The Japanese Puppet Show: 105

**Question 11(b)** — **Which exhibit interested you least?**
The 3 most frequently mentioned were:
Needlework Through the Ages: 97    The Rules of Playground Games: 73
The Spinning Top Exhibition: 74

**Question 12** — **What other attractions do you think the museum should feature?**
The 3 most frequently mentioned were:
Computer games: 196    Football: 54
More activities/things to do: 117

**Question 13(a)** — **Did you use the following at the museum?**
Free leaflet: 499    Guide book: 118
Directional signs: 369

**Question 13(b)** — **How helpful did you find them?**

|  | very good | good | average | poor | very poor |
|---|---|---|---|---|---|
| Leaflet | 151 | 195 | 107 | 39 | 7 |
| Guide book | 41 | 51 | 14 | 11 | 1 |
| Directional signs | 21 | 70 | 149 | 106 | 56 |

**Question 14** — **How would you rate the following?**

|  | very good | good | average | poor | very poor |
|---|---|---|---|---|---|
| Staff | 175 | 188 | 118 | 67 | 14 |
| Shop | 58 | 104 | 172 | 98 | 70 |
| Parking facilities | 11 | 44 | 125 | 108 | 63 |
| Labelling of exhibits | 197 | 136 | 175 | 44 | 10 |

**Question 15** — **What other suggestions for facilities or services do you have?**
The 5 most frequently mentioned were:
Snack bar/catering outlet: 172    Larger car park: 47
More modern games and toys: 91    Leaflets/guide books designed for children: 29
More activities/trying things out: 66

**2** What recommendations would you make for improving customer care and the products and services at the Museum?

# 3.10 American Express (Travel-Related Services division): evaluating customer care

**Develops knowledge and understanding of the following element:**

**4**    Evaluate the operation of a customer care programme.

**Supports the development of the following core skills:**

Communication level 3: Prepare written material; Read and respond to written material and images (Task 1)

Communication level 3: Prepare written material; Application of number level 3: Gather and process data; Interpret and present mathematical data (Task 2)

In addition to its well known financial operations American Express is a major provider of **retail travel**. The company has always stressed the quality of the service it provides. The values of the company (known internally as Blue Box values, after the company logo) are based on principles which emphasise integrity, teamwork, quality, community and, above all, the importance of the customer. This means that providing an outstanding service to customers is fundamental to the way the company's business is planned and run.

Evaluating customer care accurately requires the establishment of standards against which performance can be measured. Some of these standards may be measurable, for example the time it takes to answer telephone enquiries, while others, like the way face-to-face customers are greeted, may be more difficult to quantify. Nevertheless the skill of greeting customers correctly can be broken down into a number of basic requirements. American Express employees are expected to:

- make eye contact
- smile when greeting the customer
- use their name when it is known
- ask open questions with enthusiasm.

*American Express is a major provider of retail travel.*

Targets can be set for telephone answering. These will generally take account of past experience to set a percentage of calls which should be answered within ten seconds of being received. A target may also be set showing the maximum percentage acceptable for calls where the caller hangs up or is lost in transfer. One way of evaluating the quality of the answers given to customers on the telephone is to suggest standard formats for the most common types of enquiry. This is often a matter of identifying appropriate information and recording it. Some companies use a **pro forma** which acts as a prompt to sales staff and ensures that they include all relevant details. American Express includes in its quality standard for answering the telephone correctly a requirement that important information is recapped at the end of the call.

Some elements of customer care seem too obvious to need stating, but they can still be overlooked. Anyone who comes into a travel agency to browse, for example, should be offered assistance. The majority will want some attention and advice, even if this is in their own time. An exchange of information is important even when a sale is not made immediately, since it may help to provide a more prompt and efficient service if the customer returns.

With more complicated sales, such as business or leisure travel, **documentation** will provide further evidence of the quality of customer care. It should be comprehensible, complete and provided sufficiently in advance of departure. Any special conditions or amendments should be clearly understood. American Express produces a check list for the documentation to be sent out to customers who have made travel reservations with them. A company quality standard states that 100% of such documentation should be complete and accurate. Weekly checks are carried out to monitor how consistently this standard is being achieved. The final travel tickets and details have to be delivered within an agreed time limit.

Any company seeking to provide an above-average service to customers will probably aim to add features which the customer is likely to see as extras. Airlines, for example, have frequently offered free gifts such as wash bags to first class passengers. American Express offers a range of additional information to travellers, while guides, gifts or complimentary foreign currency are offered to higher spenders.

Handling complaints is an important part of customer care. American Express argues that complaining customers are valuable in that they enable the company to put things right. If the complaint is dealt with promptly and in a constructive manner, the loyalty of the customer to the company can still be established. Early acknowledgement of the complaint and on-going information about progress in dealing with it are indications of good quality service. Wherever possible the response should be personal and not simply a standard form.

## Your tasks

I A local travel agency, Pip's Trips Limited, has circulated a questionnaire to its customers. A question about the quality of service provided resulted in the following responses:

  a) 'When I came in all the reps were busy, so I sat down to wait. Just as someone got up to go another customer came through the door and the rep served them, ignoring my presence altogether....'

  b) 'The phone always seemed to be engaged when I rang. I did try in the evenings but all I got was the answer phone. I didn't leave a message because I'm hard to contact at work...'

c)  'When I insisted I wanted to go to Karpathos, because my mate had been there, the rep tried to argue. The place was nothing like I thought it would be. There was no night life at all, no proper lager, and the old folk on the beach kept wanting the ghetto blaster turned down. The whole thing was a waste of money and if you expect me to book with you again, I reckon you ought to provide me with a refund...'

d)  'I eventually received excellent advice on what was a very complicated journey, but I found the long queue very frustrating...'

e)  'I spoke to one rep on the phone and gave details of the type of holiday I wanted. I was told that they would have to check availability and would get back to me. When this didn't happen I rang again, to be told that the particular destination I had asked for was unreachable at the time of year I wanted to go'

f)  'I went into the office to explain that I was far from happy with the hotel we had been booked into. The rep was very abrupt, saying that this was not your responsibility and that I should write to the tour operator.'

Write a letter from Philip Pirrip, Managing Director of Pip's Trips, to each of the customers, acknowledging their complaints and indicating how the company intends to respond.

2  Draw up a scheme which will enable Pip's Trips Limited to assess the way it handles customer complaints. The scheme should indicate the following:

- guidelines for staff initially handling complaints
- criteria for staff investigating complaints
- methods of collecting data about complaints from customers
- methods of analysing and reporting the data collected
- agreed style and content of responses to complaints.

# Unit 4 Marketing in leisure and tourism

## 4.1 Satisfying the visitor: market research

**Develops knowledge and understanding of the following element:**
I    Identify market needs for products and services

**Supports the development of the following core skills:**
Application of number level 3: Interpret and present mathematical data (Tasks 1, 2)
Communication level 3: Prepare written material; Application of number level 3:
        Interpret and present mathematical data (Task 3)

Most visitor attractions carry out market research by distributing questionnaires to people as they leave. These are often referred to as exit surveys. The data gathered is generally incorporated into a memorandum for all departments, showing how the statistics compare with past performance and offering a comment on the trends revealed and their likely significance.

At a visitor attraction, much of the data may relate to different physical areas, sometimes using a simple rating system which asks visitors to judge how enjoyable or satisfactory they found separate features. Some surveys begin by asking visitors to indicate from a specific list of facilities the ones they expected to find before they arrived. This type of question provides the attraction with information about the general awareness which the public has of it and how accurate this is. It may reveal that some of their facilities are not well known, or that ideas of what to expect have changed over a number of years.

Providing food outlets at a major attraction requires some market research to establish whether the range and quality of the service is what customers want. Research at Churchett Hall, for example, might have shown the following:

| Whether food was brought | 1989 % | 1990 % | 1991 % | 1992 % |
|---|---|---|---|---|
| picnic | 40 | 38 | 37 | 36 |
| some snacks/drinks | 19 | 24 | 26 | 33 |
| no picnic/other food | 41 | 38 | 37 | 31 |

This showed that the proportion of visitors bringing their own snacks was rising. The marketing department would have to consider why this was. It could be that prices at existing food outlets were regarded as high, or it could be simply be that people spend less money during a recession. A further question, however, might have revealed that those who did use the food outlets judged the quality of the facilities to be very good.

Data about previous visits is particularly important in leisure and tourism. Not only are repeat visits vital to economic survival, but they also represent a previously satisfied market. Customers are already informed about what they are coming to and technically less money has had to be spent on advertising in order to attract them.

Suppose that research at two contrasting attractions showed the following patterns of repeat visits:

| Number of previous visits to Churchett Hall (%) | 1989 % | 1990 % | 1991 % | 1992 % |
|---|---|---|---|---|
| none | 52 | 44 | 54 | 45 |
| one | 21 | 24 | 15 | 14 |
| two or three | 17 | 20 | 20 | 28 |
| four or more | 6 | 12 | 10 | 13 |

| Number of previous visits to Aylott Park (%) | 1990 % | 1991 % | 1992 % |
|---|---|---|---|
| none | 36 | 28 | 25 |
| one or more | 64 | 72 | 75 |

These figures show a rise in the proportion of repeat visitors to Churchett Hall and Aylott Park. The two sets of data show some of the difficulties of drawing comparisons:
- figures for 1989 are not available for both attractions
- questions in the surveys asked the respondents to discriminate differently about the number of their previous visits.

This means, for example, that it is possible to conclude from these figures that three quarters of the visitors to Aylott Park have been once before, but it is also possible that the same proportion have all been three times before. When viewing this data you should also take into consideration points such as the location of the two attractions and the radius from within which they attract the majority of their visitors. Suppose the journey times to the two attractions were as shown in the following tables:

| Journey time to Churchett Hall | 1988 % | 1989 % | 1990 % | 1991 % | 1992 % |
|---|---|---|---|---|---|
| 0-½ hour | 36 | 36 | 33 | 33 | 25 |
| 1½ hour | 34 | 35 | 37 | 37 | 38 |
| 1-½ hours | 20 | 17 | 18 | 17 | 21 |
| 1½-2 hours | 9 | 9 | 9 | 10 | 13 |
| 2 hours or more | 1 | 1 | 3 | 3 | 3 |

| Journey time to Aylott Park 1992 (groups only) | % |
|---|---|
| 0-1hour | 23 |
| 1-½ hours | 29 |
| 1½-2 hours | 32 |
| 2-2½ hours | 12 |
| 2½ hours or more | 4 |

Again the data is reported in a slightly different way which restricts the amount of direct comparison. There is a clear trend showing that more visitors are coming to Churchett Hall from further afield. However, Aylott Park still has a wider geographical appeal, with a much higher proportion of visitors travelling for more than two hours to get there.

Market research surveys may ask respondents about their television viewing habits, the newspapers they read or whether they listen regularly to commercial radio. The purpose of such questions is to establish the most appropriate **media** for future advertising campaigns. Similarly a question which establishes profiles of visitors, by age and social class for example, indicates which markets the attraction is successfully penetrating.

### Your tasks

Study the following table about the types of parties visiting a popular leisure park:

|  | 1989 % | 1990 % | 1991 % | 1992 % |
|---|---|---|---|---|
| individual/'on my own' | 0 | 0 | 0 | 3 |
| adults without children | 19 | 22 | 32 | 38 |
| one parent with children | 12 | 10 | 9 | 9 |
| both parents with children | 42 | 35 | 27 | 25 |
| 2 or more women with children | 7 | 3 | 6 | 5 |
| other adult(s) with child(ren) | 20 | 30 | 26 | 20 |

1  Discuss the trends that can be identified from this data.

2  Give possible explanations for the trends you have found.

3  Write a short memorandum for all departments within the leisure park suggesting what implications these figures might have for 1993.

# 4.2 Marketing tourism: information technology

**Develops knowledge and understanding of the following element:**
2    Identify market opportunities

**Supports the development of the following core skills:**
Application of number level 3: Interpret and present mathematical data (Tasks 1, 2)

Computing and telecommunications have already made a significant impact on leisure and tourism, especially in the travel industry. Computers have been used for some time to store such information as airline seat availability and prices. Sophisticated computer reservations systems (often known simply as CRS) like Sabre can store as many as 50 million fares and handle over 2000 transactions per second. Travel agents can make bookings in a fraction of the time it used to take when they had to telephone airlines and tour operators for basic information. The development of advanced telecommunications systems also means that sales and marketing information can be **networked** to sales staff and customers around the world extremely rapidly.

Tourism businesses may not, however, always be in a position to take advantage of these developments. Placing information about a business or a tourist destination or service on a CRS is expensive. The development costs can be high and charges are made to those doing business through the systems. The provision of data for a CRS is in any case only a part of the marketing process: it does not guarantee that the customers who might be interested in purchasing the product actually get to see the information about it. Nor does it guarantee they will buy it even if they do get access to the right information. Placing information about your business on a CRS also hands a degree of control over bookings and purchases to other users of the system, such as travel agents. Owners of small businesses may in particular be reluctant to give up altogether their control over the type of custom they attract.

Destinations such as seaside resorts with large numbers of small guest houses and self-catering apartments might find that their range of accommodation was less successfully represented on CRSs than destinations with many large international hotels. So counter staff in travel agents outside the immediate area might find that they had more access to information about resorts with large international hotels than to those with small guest houses and self-catering apartments.

According to Gilbert Archdale, writing in the Tourism Society's bulletin, the answer to the problem of destinations wishing to maintain their share of the market despite their dependence on small tourism businesses lies with destination databases. These would link the existing databases of products, like tours and attractions, with databases containing customer information and with CRSs. It would help the travel agent to establish a swift and automatic link between the customers' interests and needs and the most suitable destinations. Without such developments there is every chance that holiday choices will continue to be controlled by tour operators and airlines.

## Your tasks

The information in the following tables is taken from market analysis prepared by a company called CCN Marketing Ltd for use by the Co-op Travelcare Service. It deals with some of the leisure activities of the residents of the towns of Rhyl and Abingdon.

Information Technology has been used to analyse data taken from, among other sources, the National Census. Computer calculations enable the figures for Rhyl and Abingdon to be compared rapidly with the national totals (referred to as the base).

The third pair of columns is perhaps of most interest to marketing departments. The concept of penetration offers them a means of assessing the extent to which a known group of people differs from the average. This can be applied to their knowledge of a product or, as in this case, to aspects of their tastes and lifestyles. The last column in these two tables (the index) shows whether the proportion of residents taking part in each leisure activity is higher or lower than the national average.

1 A company is planning to open a new sports and leisure complex and has decided that Rhyl or Abingdon might be potentially profitable sites. What evidence could they use from this data to support the choice of one town or the other as the more suitable?

2 A travel agent has offices in Rhyl and Abingdon and is considering promotions of the following holidays in both branches:
   - a budget Greek island 'sun and sand' holiday in June
   - a 3-month round the world luxury cruise
   - a 'first child free' offer for a week at a UK holiday camp in September
   - a trip to Ireland to watch the Irish Grand National
   - a 10-day gourmet tour of France.

Using data from the analysis, how could you best advise the agent as to which holiday to promote in each town?

## Analysis of the leisure activities of the residents of Rhyl

Title: Leisure data

Target zone: 5 km radius of Rhyl

Client: Co-operative Wholesale Society

Base zone: Great Britain (national)

| | Target zone | | Base zone | | Target/base | |
|---|---|---|---|---|---|---|
| | Count | Ratio | Count | Ratio | Penetration | Index |
| **Household data** | | | | | | |
| Total 1989 households | 15 519 | 100.0% | 22 012 432 | 100% | 0.00071 | 100 |
| **Holidays** | | | | | | |
| Beach/resort holiday last year | 3300 | 21.3% | 4 806 745 | 21.8% | 0.00069 | 97 |
| 2 or more holidays last year | 4212 | 27.1% | 5 823 388 | 26.5% | 0.00072 | 103 |
| Last holiday less than £250 | 4332 | 27.9% | 6 010 680 | 27.3% | 0.00072 | 102 |
| Last holiday more than £1000 | 829 | 5.3% | 1 227 426 | 5.6% | 0.00068 | 96 |
| Flown in the last 3 years | 6928 | 44.6% | 9 424 961 | 42.8% | 0.00074 | 104 |
| **Population data** | | | | | | |
| Total 1989 population | 38 483 | 100.0% | 55 310 568 | 100.0% | 0.00070 | 100 |
| **Social activities** | | | | | | |
| Visit restaurants once a month | 4512 | 11.7% | 6 633 672 | 12.0% | 0.00068 | 98 |
| Visit pubs 2-3 times a week | 5148 | 13.4% | 7 740 843 | 14.0% | 0.00067 | 96 |
| Play bingo at club regularly | 2218 | 5.8% | 3 700 292 | 6.7% | 0.00060 | 86 |
| Keep fit regularly | 3845 | 10.0% | 49 960 84 | 9.0% | 0.00077 | 111 |
| **Television viewing** | | | | | | |
| Watch American football | 5274 | 13.7% | 7 856 216 | 14.2% | 0.00067 | 96 |
| Watch soccer | 11 128 | 28.9% | 16 959 980 | 30.7% | 0.00066 | 94 |
| Watch cricket | 9196 | 23.9% | 12 839 606 | 23.2% | 0.00072 | 103 |
| Watch horse racing | 4909 | 12.8% | 7 129 368 | 12.9% | 0.00069 | 99 |
| Watch wrestling | 5440 | 14.1% | 8 291 222 | 15.0% | 0.00066 | 94 |

*continued overleaf*

## Analysis of the leisure activities of the residents of Abingdon

Title: Leisure data
Target zone: 5 km radius of Abingdon

Client: Co-operative Wholesale Society
Base zone: Great Britain (target)

| | Target zone | | Base zone | | Target/base | |
|---|---|---|---|---|---|---|
| | Count | Ratio | Count | Ratio | Penetration | Index |
| **Household data** | | | | | | |
| Total 1989 households | 19 309 | 100.0% | 22 013 696 | 100% | 0.00088 | 100 |
| **Holidays** | | | | | | |
| Beach/resort holiday last year | 4571 | 23.7% | 4 806 986 | 21.8% | 0.00095 | 108 |
| 2 or more holidays last year | 5985 | 31.0% | 5 823 783 | 26.5% | 0.00103 | 117 |
| Last holiday less than £250 | 5427 | 28.1% | 60 110 53 | 27.3% | 0.00090 | 103 |
| Last holiday more than £1000 | 1455 | 7.5% | 1 227 516 | 5.6% | 0.00119 | 135 |
| Flown in the last 3 years | 9425 | 48.8% | 9 425 585 | 42.8% | 0.00100 | 114 |
| **Population data** | | | | | | |
| Total 1989 population | 53 164 | 100.0% | 55 313 668 | 100.0% | 0.00096 | 100 |
| **Social activities** | | | | | | |
| Visit restaurants once a month | 7412 | 13.9% | 66 340 67 | 12.0% | 0.00112 | 116 |
| Visit pubs 2-3 times a week | 7238 | 13.6% | 7 741 248 | 14.0% | 0.00093 | 97 |
| Play bingo at club regularly | 2337 | 4.4% | 3 700 410 | 6.7% | 0.00063 | 66 |
| Keep fit regularly | 4972 | 9.4% | 4996352 | 9.0% | 0.00100 | 104 |
| **Television viewing** | | | | | | |
| Watch American football | 7926 | 14.9% | 7 856 617 | 14.2% | 0.00101 | 105 |
| Watch soccer | 15 820 | 29.8% | 16 960 932 | 30.7% | 0.00093 | 97 |
| Watch cricket | 13 219 | 24.9% | 12 840 417 | 23.2% | 0.00103 | 107 |
| Watch horse racing | 6084 | 11.4% | 7 129 734 | 12.9% | 0.00085 | 89 |
| Watch wrestling | 7216 | 13.6% | 8 291 590 | 15.0% | 0.00087 | 91 |

# 4.3 Marketing *A Day at the Wells*

**Develops knowledge and understanding of the following element:**

**2**    Identify market opportunities

**Supports the development of the following core skill:**

Communication level 3: Read and respond to written material and images (Tasks 1, 2, 3)

Marketing an attraction is intended to increase its number of visitors and hence its revenue. In order to be successful it needs to convince potential visitors that the attraction is good value for money. Good marketing can also benefit the destination as a whole, attracting people from outside to spend money there.

A *Day at the Wells* is a tourist attraction in Tunbridge Wells. It consists of an exhibition in the town's renovated Corn Exchange, recreating a summer's day in the town as it might have been in 1740. There are scenes representing, among other things, a stage coach departure, a coffee house and a candlelit ball.

The first concern in marketing an attraction such as this is to identify the **target markets**. These might include:

- the travel trade
- ferry operators
- organisers of educational visits
- local residents
- groups with an interest in Georgian or local history
- local companies looking for interesting conference venues.

The next decision to be made is how best to communicate with these target markets. Though the best known means of doing this is by advertising, there are other ways of increasing public awareness of the attraction:

- good press and public relations can ensure coverage of events and new developments within the attraction
- joint promotions, run with companies like British Rail, may attract new visitors by offering special concessions
- being represented at trade exhibitions offers the attraction the opportunity to persuade tour operators to include it in the itinerary of some of their tours
- good signs in the local area mean that casual visitors to Tunbridge Wells are more likely to be drawn towards *A Day at the Wells*
- the use of costumed actors on the surrounding streets can arouse the curiosity of potential visitors.

*A Day at the Wells* is only one of a number of attractions marketed by a company called Heritage Projects. Others include *The Oxford Story, The Canterbury Tales,* and *The White Cliffs Experience.* Joint marketing of these attractions means that the same target markets can be reached more cost effectively. All of these attractions conduct exit surveys in order to find out more about the kind of people they are attracting. These surveys ask where visitors have come from, how they came to hear of the attraction, and what they thought of various aspects of their experience. Many of the questions are designed to produce short answers which will provide quantitative data. In other words, the attractions will be able to draw conclusions about such things as the percentage of visitors who come from within a radius of two hours' travelling time.

Most marketing departments will have a computer database of contacts and addresses for direct mail. These mean that the user can select the particular target market – for example, coach operators or schools – and only print out addresses to these. This is more cost effective than sending every promotion to all addresses on the database. Attractions will often use sophisticated analyses of residential areas in order to pinpoint the type of market they hope to reach. If *A Day at the Wells* decides that its main market is people in social income groups A, B, and C1 and old-age pensioners, most of them coming from the South East, it can pay a research company to come up with suggested clusters of housing likely to provide the highest concentration of such people.

The medium chosen and the style of communicating are also important. If exit surveys suggest that people visiting *A Day at the Wells* do so primarily for entertainment, leaflets and television advertising would reflect this fact by aiming at a relatively light-hearted approach. *The Oxford Story*, on the other hand, probably attracts more visitors seeking background information about the city's history, so this is reflected in leaflets advertising the attraction. *The White Cliffs Experience* did not attract many visitors in hot weather since it was seen solely as an indoor attraction. Yet it proved possible to extend its market

*Period costume on show at A Day at The Wells*

by organising a programme of outdoor events there.

It is important to get the pricing policy right if visitors are to be persuaded to come to an attraction. There are several general relevant factors. Attractions like Chessington World of Adventures, whose main market is families with children aged up to 14, are aware that the price of admission needs to fall within most families' idea of a budget for a day out. Setting too high a cost for the whole family may mean that one parent will opt out of the visit and go for a stroll or a cup of tea! It may be that certain prices represent psychological barriers, so that though people are willing to pay £9.99 for something they will not pay over £10. Another factor in the pricing policy of an individual attraction will be charges made by competitors. It can either aim to undercut them, or to demonstrate that the attraction offers an experience of a higher quality which is worth paying more for. The overall economic climate will have a bearing too, in that it is more difficult to raise admission charges during a recession. Pricing will also depend on the policy of the attraction's owners. Where attractions have been partly funded by the local council, as with The White Cliffs Experience, or where some of the directors of a project are also local councillors, as with the Dome in Doncaster, the pricing policy will need to take account of the overall council strategy for the area.

Not all revenue from an attraction comes from admission charges. Retailing is increasingly used as a feature of indoor attractions like *A Day at the Wells*, offering gifts, local books and souvenirs as reminders of the visit. Some attractions employ active retailing. For example, at *The Tales of Robin Hood* visitors can have a lesson in firing a bow and arrow. They can then move on to a shop within the attraction where, among other items, bows and arrows are for sale.

Attractions like Chessington World of Adventures which use regional television advertising as their main means of promotion will also need to evaluate the effects of each campaign, to ensure that they are worth the investment. They employ an outside agency to conduct carefully structured interviews to test people's awareness of the advertisements shown. High recall of the content suggests the campaign is succeeding. Chessington would need to ensure that its adverts were shown between programmes likely to appeal especially to the 8-14 age group. Television advertising space can be purchased at different rates, mainly dependent on the anticipated number of viewers at the intended slot. A particular time can only be guaranteed if the highest rates are paid. At other times a potential advertiser can be pre-empted by someone offering a higher sum for the same slot.

## Your tasks

Read the text from the leaflet advertising *A Day at the Wells* on the following page and then answer the following questions:

1  How many different markets is the leaflet intended to appeal to

2  What different techniques have been used to try to appeal to each of these different markets?

3  Find each of the following words used the text:
   brilliantly, elegant, scandalous, authentic, congenial, gentlemen, aphrodisiac, glamorous.
   Discuss why you think they were chosen instead of the following possible alternatives:
   charmingly, smart, offensive, genuine, sociable, men, love-inducing, exciting.

---

## Royal Tunbridge Wells' most elegant attraction
### A Day at the Wells: a Georgian journey

Entertaining and educational, A Day at the Wells brilliantly recreates a summer's day in 1740, in the elegant and scandalous spa resort of Tunbridge Wells.

The exhibition, acclaimed for its authentic scenes and lifelike models, takes you on a journey into the past, starting from a coaching inn in Southwark where the stage coach is about to leave for Tunbridge Wells

A typical day at 'the Wells' unfolds: a congenial coffee for gentlemen in the Coffee house; a stroll for the ladies along The Pantiles to see and be seen; a glass of the medicinal and aphrodisiac spring water said to cure almost everything, and a glamorous candlelit ball for which to prepare...

### Commentaries

There is a special commentary for children and commentaries in foreign languages are available. Arrangements have been made for the hard of hearing.

### Facilities for the disabled

We welcome visitors with impaired mobility and have access for wheelchairs. Please make an advance booking.

### Group bookings

A Day at the Wells is perfect for group visits. A pre-booked group is offered a 10 per cent reduction on the normal admission price. Trade Manual and Group information are available on request.

Evening viewing can be arranged for groups and refreshments provided. A Day at the Wells holds an alcohol licence.

A spacious hospitality room provides facilities for conference delegates, corporate entertainment and special celebrations.

### Gift shop

A separate shop offers a wonderful selection of individual gifts, local books and souvenirs.

### Educational services

A Teachers' Resource Pack, containing suggestions for activities based on the exhibition, is available. Together with work based on historical topics and local studies, the pack suggests follow-up activities in English, Geography, Science, Maths, Technology and the Arts.

A fully equipped education room is available and our education officer is on site to give advice and help where necessary.

# 4.4 Predicting leisure markets

**Develops knowledge and understanding of the following element:**
**2**    Identify market opportunities

**Supports the development of the following core skills:**
Communication level 3: Take part in discussions; Application of number level 3: Gather and process data (Task 1)
Application of number level 3: Gather and process data (Task 2)

New leisure developments will have to be aware of changing social attitudes and changing technology if they are to be successful. For example, there is likely to be growing opposition in the UK to the use of green field sites for large leisure complexes. Increased awareness of environmental issues may strengthen the movement towards creating both enclosed and simulated leisure environments. These can reduce the direct impact of people on the landscape, and at the same time reduce the amount of travelling they have to do to satisfy their leisure interests.

Many existing leisure facilities depend on a single activity, as in the case of a football ground or a cinema. Their use is therefore limited and they can only be adapted for either outdoor or indoor activities. Future leisure facilities are more likely to be complexes offering a range of activities, appealing to a range of interests and age groups. They will look for ways of attracting visitors at all times of year and in all weathers. This means seeking to appeal to different markets, for example

- business users
- cultural interests
- education
- exhibitions
- conventions.

This will in turn present designers with a challenge. Some existing leisure centres are sufficiently flexible to be capable of use as convention centres, concert halls and indoor sports venues.

Providing leisure facilities is not only about attracting high-spending visitors into a community: local needs and views will have to be taken into account in future plans. A willingness to involve the local community in the planning process can have a double advantage:

- it may make planning permission easier to acquire
- it can also encourage the local people to have a positive attitude to
  leisure developments.

Changes in holiday habits, travel systems and work customs will need to be closely monitored by tomorrow's leisure providers. There is likely to be an increase in the current trend towards more short breaks and the demand for leisure facilities close to **source markets**. Possible reasons for this are:

- foreign travel may be seen as   expensive by some and potentially harmful by others
- traffic congestion and increased air and rail fares may reduce the distances people are willing to travel.

*Two uses of a flexible leisure space*

Changes in people's working lives will also affect the leisure market. For example, the combination of earlier retirement, redundancy and increased life expectancy means that the leisure demands of the over-50 age group will rise very rapidly.

A study of retailing may offer some pointers to leisure developers, particularly since many would say that shopping has become a major leisure activity. As major retailers have developed marketing strategies, in order to establish their distinctiveness from each other they have had to treat customers as increasingly discriminating. This has led to a greater range of products being made available, more services such as carry out systems and cash provision being added, and an acknowledgement of public concerns about, for example, health or the environment. The discriminating leisure consumer will expect the same quality – a range of services, an acceptable level of convenience and an acknowledgement of their opinions and lifestyle.

Future leisure marketing will no doubt make greater use of technology. Advertising leisure facilities through television or newspapers is very undirected. Customer databases are a more accurate way of aiming marketing material at the audience most likely to be receptive to it. Teletext systems offer one route of more accurately matching up customer and product. If the theory that customers will become more discriminating proves accurate, teletext is able to provide accurate up-to-date information on leisure facilities and services. Assuming that they will also demand greater convenience, the facility to make advanced bookings through the same system should be a high priority.

## Your tasks

1 Discuss both the existing and unfulfilled leisure demands of your own student group, in terms of range of provision, location, cost, and time.
   Canvass the views of parents or guardians about the leisure provision available when they were in their late teens.
   Compare the provision available to the two generations. What are the main changes which have taken place?

2 Use your own observation and research to estimate the demand for leisure in your local area.
   Prepare a profile of what you think is the likely potential leisure market in the immediate vicinity of your school or college.

**77**

You might consider some of the following:
- employment patterns
- apparent affluence
- car ownership levels
- public transport systems
- existing leisure provision
- levels of use of existing leisure facilities
- questionnaire responses.

# 4.5 Marketing national parks

**Develops knowledge and understanding of the following element:**

**3**    Plan promotional activities

**Supports the development of the following core skill:**

Communication level 3: Prepare written material (Tasks 1, 2)

The leisure and tourism industries place a heavy emphasis on successful marketing. Attractions and facilities compete with each other for visitors, but the product being sold is generally more complex than something people buy in a shop. While a souvenir may be judged in terms of its workmanship or aesthetic appeal, the visit during which it was bought will be judged in terms of the whole experience. This may include travel, accommodation, landscape, services and facilities. Planning the marketing of a souvenir is therefore always going to be simpler than the marketing of a destination.

Marketing a tourist destination becomes particularly difficult when there are a number of different attractions within a well defined area such as a national park. Many visitors will be touring the region rather than stopping in a single location. The first priority is usually to define the characteristics of the region which make it distinctive.

The Countryside Commission suggests that there are four ways in which individual enterprises can successfully improve their marketing:

- Obtaining accurate information about visitors is essential: knowing where they have come from, why they came, where they heard about the area and what they enjoyed or disliked about their visits can help individual leisure and tourism centres to plan ahead.
- Using this information to target markets lessens the chances of advertisements and direct mail failing to reach sympathetic audiences.
- Making sure that people enjoy their visits is a factor in good marketing. If people go away happy, they are more likely to make repeat visits and to be receptive to information about new developments in the region.
- Seeking professional advice, whether from a regional tourist board or a marketing company, may ultimately generate more visitors as a result of a specific campaign or promotion.

Many leisure and tourism businesses, such as a bed and breakfast hotel or a boat hire com-

*Yorkshire Dales
National Park:
Malham Cove*

pany, are small operations. This means they do not have the funds for the more expensive kinds of promotion like glossy brochures or television advertising. However they can often benefit from group marketing. The National Farm Holiday Bureau for example co-ordinates the work of separate farm holiday groups in each of the national parks. Not only does this enable small enterprises to pool resources, but also to work jointly on creating common booking systems and developing tours and packages designed to appeal to specific markets.

One way of attracting and retaining visitors to areas like national parks is to provide them with a range of activities. These need to be locally available, clearly signed and well researched. They might also include instruction and demonstration in various skills and techniques. The Countryside Commission describes four ways of using these activities in marketing the area:

- send out information on these opportunities before arrival, or to past visitors. This might involve consulting with the national park authority in selecting particular events to promote
- put together and promote simple packages involving some of these activities, based on weekend breaks or longer stays, including off-season periods
- put together a walking or cycling package between a number of accommodation enterprises, with visitors' luggage transported between them
- work with other tourism enterprises, the national parks authority and other agencies to devise a comprehensive programme of walks, lectures, conservation work, etc., to give a varied and imaginative insight into the national park.

## Your tasks

1 Identify a renovation or conservation scheme in need of voluntary labour. List the activities at the site which require labour and identify the skills which might be particularly useful.

Plan a programme of activities for visitors willing to spend part of their holiday in the region working on the scheme. The programme should indicate:

- the mix of work and leisure
- the accommodation to be used
- how the scheme is to be funded.

2  Design a leaflet, to be distributed in colleges and universities, which is intended to attract students to spend their summer vacations working on the project.

# 4.6 Presenting marketing plans for new products 1

**Develops knowledge and understanding of the following element:**

3     Plan promotional activities

**Supports the development of the following core skills:**

Communication level 3: Take part in discussions (Task 1)

Communication level 3: Prepare written material (Task 2)

## Introduction and background

A good marketing plan must be both feasible and based on well researched data. It needs to explain the background of the marketing idea and its objectives. It should indicate the research methods employed and the data used in forming a marketing strategy. The strategy itself is often described under four headings: product, place, price and promotion. No marketing plan would be complete without a budget statement itemising the plan's predicted costs.

The background to a marketing plan should explain how the idea for a new product or service came about and why it is appropriate at a particular time and in a particular area. The current popularity of a particular television series, for example, might be a reason for promoting themed short break holidays in the town or region where the series is set. The introduction to the plan could also discuss people's general spending habits in the region, suggesting why it is thought that there is a gap in the market. There should also be some general consideration both of the potential competition and of the likely stimuli for new products or services.

Marketing objectives may be either short term or long term. Short term objectives could involve piloting the new idea to see whether it needed modifying in any way. Certainly they would include identifying target markets and planning a marketing campaign. Short term objectives can also be very specific (such as finding out which three flavours of seaside rock are most popular) or they can be much broader, as in the case of a new Tourist Information Centre whose objective was to raise the profile of a specific destination. Long term objectives are also likely to contain broad statements about anticipated achievement. They could relate to quality of services or products or changes in public perceptions. Some objectives will have a commercial basis, for example they may refer to sales targets or increasing the frequency of visitors.

It is important in the marketing plan to provide an early assessment of the merits and possible weaknesses of the proposal. This is sometimes achieved by means of a SWOT analysis. This is a simple method of deciding whether a marketing idea is worth pursuing by listing its strengths, weaknesses, opportunities and threats. A company planning to market themed Sherlock Holmes weekends in London, for example, might produce a SWOT analysis which looked something like this:

**Strengths**
- Sherlock Holmes is an internationally known name.
- The subject has always been associated with London.
- No similar weekend break is currently available.
- Overseas visitors to London frequently inquire about Holmes.
- London offers a wide range of additional attractions.

**Weaknesses**
- Most places mentioned in the Holmes stories have lost their Victorian appearance.
- Tour parties in busy London streets have to be kept small.
- Attractions directly relating to Holmes are few in number.
- The market is limited to those with an interest in Sherlock Holmes.

**Opportunities**
- Sherlock Holmes stories have been recently serialised on television, showing both in the UK and overseas.
- Some historical aspects of Central London have not been fully exploited.

**Threats**
- The British weather!
- Perceived risks, especially by overseas visitors, of terrorist bomb attacks.
- The economic recession and unfavourable exchange rates.
- Competition from other tourist attractions.

**Your tasks**

1 Identify a single new product or service which you think might exploit a gap in the leisure and/or tourism markets. Devise a number of short term and long term objectives for marketing the product or service.
Discuss the factors which would control how successfully each of these objectives would be met.

2 Select one of the following proposals:
- an East Enders theme park in East London
- a Vietnamese Restaurant in a small town or village near where you live
- a dance studio in a mining village.
Write a SWOT analysis for the proposal you have chosen.

# 4.7 Presenting marketing plans for new products 2

**Develops knowledge and understanding of the following element:**
3   Plan promotional activities

**Supports the development of the following core skill:**
Application of number level 3: Interpret and present mathematical data (Tasks 1, 2, 3, 4, 5)

# Product, price, promotion, place

Products may be material objects such as goods sold in shops. In leisure and tourism, however, they are just as likely to be services, such as sports and entertainment ticket reservation services, the provision of restaurant meals, combinations of transport, facilities and accommodation or services creating excursions or tours.

If the new product was a themed break, the marketing plan would have to propose a detailed itinerary for potential customers. Details like transfers to and from airports or railway stations, timings of meals, roles to be played by guides and outside speakers, and any special clothing or equipment required would form part of the product description. The positive aspects of the product need to be emphasised if the company or a bank are to be persuaded to invest in it. Some aspects of the plan may require justification, for instance the decision to accommodate people in a particularly expensive hotel. In schemes where activities are involved, the plan may need to provide relevant detail about locations, safety, transport, special clothing and equipment and any extra costs.

However good the product, the marketing will not be effective if the price is unrealistic. Any scheme will have to cover all the *fixed* costs before a profit can be made. In the case of a themed break the fixed costs would include some transport costs like coach hire, and some fixed service costs, such as fees for guides and speakers. The *variable* costs would include accommodation and meals. These would vary according to the number of people actually taking the break. The money received from each person will exceed the average cost of the product or service and that difference will represent the profit to be made. The plan has to calculate both the amount of profit needed to make the proposal worthwhile and viable, while at the same time estimating what potential purchasers will regard as value for money.

Promotion is the part of the marketing plan intended to increase demand for the product. The type of promotion featured will depend largely on the target market, though cost will also be a factor. There would be more point in advertising a new cricketing holiday to Corfu in Cricket Monthly than in The Angling Times. Planning a new leisure centre in Penzance might involve direct mail as a means of promotion, but the letters would only be sent to those within reasonable travelling distance of the proposed development. Advertising in the national press or on television may have the advantage of reaching a very wide audience, but it may also be far more costly than the likely revenue from the scheme could justify. The majority of readers or viewers may in any case fall outside the market segments likely to be interested in the product.

In order to reach defined target markets, the plan must show how and where promotional materials are to be distributed. Brochures about new tourist attractions, for example, might be distributed from tourist information centres, travel agents, public libraries and hotels in the same region. They could, however, also be distributed outside the region through places like railway stations and at travel trade exhibitions and fairs. Tour operators might be persuaded to include the brochure in information packs sent out to customers booking tours in the region.

## Your tasks

Look at the figures on the opposite page which give the fixed and variable costs of a proposed weekend holiday package based on a Sherlock Holmes theme. The package costs are calculated on the basis of thirty people taking part.

Fixed and variable costs must be covered before any profit can be made. In this instance, the package just about breaks even with the thirteenth guest. With the chosen price the **contribution margin** of £93.83 will be made on a full tour.

| Fixed costs | All figures in £ |
|---|---|
| **Apix Coaches Ltd.** | |
| 1 x whole day hire @ 175 = 175 | |
| 2 x half day hire @ 90 = 180 | 355.00 |
| **London carriages Ltd.** | |
| 6 x @ 50 per hour for 5 persons | 300.00 |
| **Livetts Launches** | |
| Cost for boat hire | 400.00 |
| **Frashards Ltd.** | |
| Waitress service for boat dinner | 35.00 |
| Tour guides and speakers | |
| 5 x @ 25 per hour | 125.00 |
| Total fixed costs | 1215.00 |

| Variable costs | All figures in £ |
|---|---|
| **Sherlock Holmes Hotel** | |
| 14 x @125 for double/twin rooms | |
| 2 x @105 for single rooms | |
| 2 nights accommodation = 3920 (10% discount for groups) | 3528.00 |
| **Frashards Ltd** | |
| 30 x @10.75 per person for buffet dinner | 322.50 |
| **Sherlock Holmes Pub** | |
| 30 x @8 per person for pub lunch = 240 (10% discount for groups) | 216.00 |
| **Golden Tours** | |
| 30 x @22 per person for show and supper | 660.00 |
| **Simpsons in The Strand** | |
| 30 x @12.50 per person for lunch = 375 (10% discount for groups) | 337.50 |
| **Sherlock Holmes Hotel** | |
| 30 x @4 per person for afternoon tea | 120.00 |
| Total variable costs | 5184.00 |
| Total costs: fixed costs | 1215.00 |
| variable costs | 5184.00 |
| | 6399.00 |
| Total cost per person | 213.30 |
| Average revenue per person | |
| (20% profit) | 266.63 |
| Total revenue | 7998.75 |

Now answer the following questions.

1 How much profit will be made on the full tour?

2 What will be the total variable costs for 30 people if discounts for groups are discontinued?

3 There are ten fully refunded cancellations, but the discounts shown are still applicable to the variable costs for the remainder of the party. At the price of £266.63 per person, what will the total revenue be?

4 If it is considered that average revenue per person cannot be increased, how many additional people would need to book beyond the first 30 to make a second tour party worthwhile? Fixed costs for the whole package double for any group size between 31 and 60.

5 No figures for office and administration overheads have been included in this example. Would these items be included as fixed or variable costs, and why?

# 4.8 Beaulieu: marketing an attraction

**Develops knowledge and understanding of the following element:**
3    Plan promotional activities

**Supports the development of the following core skills:**
Communication level 3: Take part in discussions; Read and respond to written material and images (Task 1)

Beaulieu is a highly successful visitor destination, attracting some half a million visitors each year. It offers a range of facilities, the best known of which is the National Motor Museum. In addition visitors can see the remains of the 13th century Abbey and parts of the Palace House, the Montagu family home. At nearby Buckler's Hard, on the same family estate, there are a Maritime Museum and a number of historic cottages to see.

To market the attraction successfully detailed research is carried out and analysed. An automated ticketing system can generate some initial information about visitors, showing for example, that 62 per cent are adults, 29 per cent are children and the remainder are senior citizens. About 40 per cent of the visitors come in July and August, during the main school holiday period. In addition a random sample of visitors to Beaulieu is interviewed using a standard questionnaire. Awareness surveys are also carried out in towns up to 100 miles away to try to gauge the general public's perception of Beaulieu.

This research reveals that 70 per cent of Beaulieu's visitors are holiday-makers, while the remainder are making one day excursions from home. The nearby New Forest and the seaside resort of Bournemouth are the most common points of departure for the holiday visitors. About one third of the holiday-makers stay in hotels or guest houses and a further third are on camping or caravan sites. Half the visitors come in groups including children and about a third are adult couples.

On average visitors stay four hours at Beaulieu. Almost everyone visits the most popular feature, The National Motor Museum. Research also suggests that most visitors have seen some publicity for Beaulieu before their visit, either on television or through leaflets. Visitors completing the questionnaire also indicate both the level of enjoyment the visit generated and the extent to which they felt it was value for money.

Armed with this accurate information about its visitors, the Public Relations Department is able to identify its target market. They must be people who have an interest either in the particular combination of motor, maritime and architectural history or who are keenly interested in one of these areas. The research is also important in allocating the annual marketing budget.

Once the target market has been identified, a decision is needed about the type of medium which will be most likely to make an impact yet be acceptable in terms of the cost to the company. For example, a nationwide television campaign might increase the visitor numbers but might cost more than the income generated by these extra visitors. Alternative media – such as the press, radio, journals, posters, leaflets or panels on the sides of buses – might prove to be more cost effective.

One difficulty faced by all marketers of attractions is trying to decide on the particular image they wish to put across. The public may find it easier to visualise a zoo or an art gallery than to have a clear picture of a leisure park or a mixed attraction. Many attractions began with a single focus but have since added other major features, sometimes to the extent that the original focus has become the secondary interest: Beaulieu is still best known for the Motor Museum and this will tend to feature first in general publicity but the other attractions have to be given due weight as well. The aim of the marketing will be to maximise people's enjoyment and make them fully aware of all the possibilities available to them for a single inclusive admission charge.

Securing high levels of coverage at reasonable cost is the main objective of Beaulieu's marketing. In order to achieve this a local advertising agency is employed to handle all media space bookings and to design and produce advertisements and printed publicity material.

Colour leaflets provide information for visitors. Research indicates both the kind of information visitors require and also the most sensible places to distribute the leaflets. These leaflets are available at Tourist Information Centres and holiday accommodation sites, and are also distributed by direct mail and at travel trade fairs and exhibitions. Fairs and exhibitions offer attractions like Beaulieu the opportunity to encourage tour operators and travel agents to include visits to attractions in the tour programmes they offer.

Marketing opportunities sometimes arise through working with regional and national groups involved in tourism. The Regional Tourist Board and the local councils will generally have a vested interest in promoting the region and the attractions which lie within it. Members of national organisations, such as The Treasure Houses of England, or hotel marketing consortia, such as Best Western Hotels, can help to promote each other's interests. Beaulieu maintains links

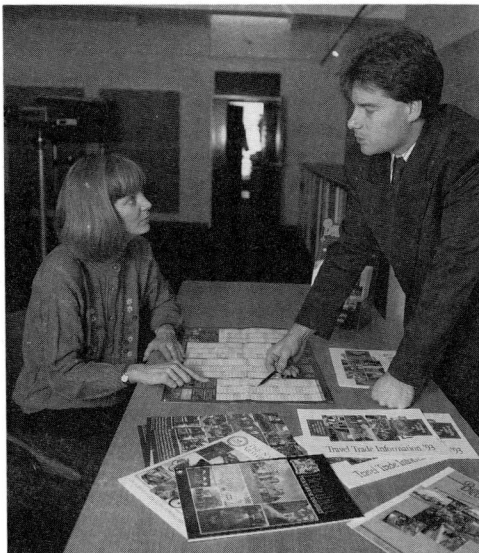

*Marketing staff at Beaulieu discussing promotional material*

**85**

with other tourist facilities in the UK, especially through a consultancy and advisory service. Though an attraction might not wish to reveal sensitive information, such as its weekly takings, to a competitor, it might share market research for example, on the grounds that this could improve the performance of both attractions.

## Your task

The previous information has been distributed to various managers at Beaulieu as the basis for a discussion of future marketing policy. In response, individual managers have highlighted the following issues and questions which could be considered in a planning meeting:

1 *The small percentage of the total number of visitors to Beaulieu made up of senior citizens:*
 - possible reasons for this
 - the type of promotional activity which might increase the percentage
 - implications of a successful promotion to this market segment.

2 *Though Beaulieu is open all year round, 40% of visitors come during July and August:*
 - the type of promotional activity which might increase visitor numbers in, say, November or February
 - the factors which would determine the budget set for such a promotional activity.

3 *Half the visitors to Beaulieu are adults with children:*
 - the extent to which this should influence media chosen for advertising and design of publicity material.

4 *The average stay at Beaulieu is four hours:*
 - should this be referred to in publicity materials?
 - what are the implications of suggesting in publicity material that Beaulieu is worth a half day's or a full day's visit ?

5 *Many attractions have added entertainment facilities, such as fairgrounds:*
 - what would be the marketing implications if such an addition were considered at Beaulieu?

6 *Posters and advertising on the sides of buses are both recognised means of gaining publicity:*
 - what advantages and disadvantages might each have as a means of publicising Beaulieu?
 - how might you calculate their cost effectiveness?

7 *Beaulieu comprises a motor museum, a 13th century abbey, a historic country house and a maritime museum:*
 - what common themes or threads can be identified to help to provide an overall picture of the various attractions?
 - how would these be best used in marketing Beaulieu?

Debate these issues in small groups. You may wish to adopt the following roles:
 - financial director
 - personnel manager
 - retail and catering manager
 - marketing and PR manager
 - Motor Museum manager
 - Buckler's Hard manager.

# 4.9 Advertising

**Develops knowledge and understanding of the following element:**

**3** Plan promotional activities

**Supports the development of the following core skills:**

Communication level 3: Read and respond to written material and images; Application of number level 3: Represent and tackle problems (Tasks 1, 2)

The main function of advertising is to make people more aware of the products or services being offered. The hope of the advertisers is that this will affect consumer choice. For example, some people will choose holiday destinations because they have featured in advertising campaigns. Others may already have decided where they want to go but will choose a Thomsons holiday rather than a Have-Fun-in-the-Sun Limited holiday because they are aware of the former company but have never heard of the latter.

Advertising has been defined as 'any paid form of non-personal presentation and promotion of ideas, products or services by an identified sponsor'. In other words it is always a commercial transaction directed by whoever is paying for it at the general public. It is used to explain what products and services are available and how these can be used. Above all, advertising aims to persuade potential buyers that a particular product or service is superior to any similar ones. Advertisers hope that the end result will be an increase in sales, particularly in the short term. A better public knowledge of the company and its products or services may enable it to increase its share of existing markets and perhaps develop new ones.

*Holiday advertising in a national newspaper*

A common system of analysing advertisements is known by the acronym AIDA: attention, interest, desire and action. This describes the process by which a good advertisement is expected to have its impact. An advertisement which fails to capture attention at the outset is unlikely to be effective. Written advertisements may use witty headlines, large print or cartoon drawings to attract attention. Television advertising is more likely to rely on a combination of striking images and distinctive soundtracks.

The message of the advertisement can only be put across fully if interest is sustained throughout. A holiday brochure may offer entrance into a prize draw for readers who extract answers from the text. A number of recent television advertisements have introduced on-going narratives based around the featured product in which the watchers are really being invited to speculate about what will happen to the relationships between the characters.

If the advertisement holds the interest but does not make the audience want to buy the service or product, the company has gained no return for its investment. Advertising is constantly seeking to latch on to common consumer motivation. Leisure advertising often focuses on the benefits of a healthy life-style. Holiday advertising may stress the need for rest and relaxation, or it may try to make people think of the aspects of their daily routine from which they would like to escape.

Consumers may of course be persuaded that they want a holiday or a healthier life-style, but this does not necessarily mean that they will go out out and spend money on them. From an advertiser's point of view the good advertisement must lead directly to actual sales. Where products are fairly similar, for example two package holidays to the same destination using similar standard accommodation, advertisers may use pricing policies as a means of persuading customers to buy. Discounts may be an inducement because people believe they are saving money. Knowing the price of something before buying it may also encourage customers, particularly those on a limited budget.

## Your tasks

Avernice Tripp Ltd, a small travel agency in Easthampton specialising in holidays to France, wishes to boost its sales in the period immediately after Christmas. The agency is considering advertising as a means of achieving this. Preliminary research has revealed the following:

### Local Press
The weekly Easthampton Gazette has a circulation of 25 000 and charges £225 for each quarter-page advertisement.

### Local Radio
Listen East, the local radio station, claims it can be received in 50 000 homes, though local research suggests only 20 per cent listen regularly. A two-minute advertising slot at a favourable time costs £400.

### Regional Television
ETV, the regional independent channel, gives access to 120 000 homes, though only a third of these are in Easthampton itself. A 30-second advertisement would cost £750, but would cost £4 000 to make.

### Direct Mail
A local direct mail company, using information built up from credit records, will send out promotional letters designed and printed by the advertisers at £350 per 1000. Writing

and printing the promotional material would add a further £1250 to the cost.

1 Given that Avernice Tripp Ltd makes an average profit of £40 on each holiday sold, how much extra business do you think they would need to generate to make each of the four listed methods of advertising worthwhile?

2 What do you think would be the benefits and potential risks of each of these four methods of advertising?

Which single medium do you think would most effectively meet the company's needs? What reasons can you give to support this view?

3 Avernice Tripp Limited is particularly concerned that they are losing customers to a small specialist tour operator in the town, Vacances Jacques. This company specialises in self-catering accommodation and has been undercutting Avernice Tripp's prices for similar holidays.

Present a plan for a promotion specifically aimed at enabling Tripps to ward off this competition.

# 4.10 Advertising law and codes

**Develops knowledge and understanding of the following element:**

3     Plan promotional activities

**Supports the development of the following core skills:**

Communication level 3: Read and respond to written material and images (Task 1)
Communication level 3: Take part in discussions (Task 2)
Communication level 3: Read and respond to written material and images (Task 3)
Communication level 3: Take part in discussions (Task 4)
Communication level 3: Prepare written material (Task 5)

Trading standards departments receive about 26 000 complaints each year about holidays. Some of these are the result of companies going out of business, but many are related to undeclared surcharges or taxes or substandard accommodation and facilities. Trading standards officers have the role of ensuring that companies keep within the law when they advertise.

A holiday brochure, as with other items covered by the 1968 Trades Descriptions Act, must not make false claims. Facilities at the resort should be accurately described and the correct photographs shown. The full price, with no hidden additions, should be clearly shown. The 1987 Consumer Protection Act makes it an offence to mislead consumers about the price of goods for sale. If a holiday cannot be sold without insurance, the cost of the policy must be included when the price is quoted to the customer. The small print may protect the company from liability against some unforeseen circumstances but any conditions they impose must be reasonable and clear. The Unfair Contract Terms Act of 1977 gives consumers protection against an unfair contract, for example one which attempted to disclaim any liability on the part of a tour operator for personal injuries resulting from their negligence.

The 1993 European Community package travel directive is more specific than the Trades Descriptions Act. It gives the consumer greater power to take civil action against a travel company, even where the small print would appear to deny this right. The directive does not, however, give trading standards officers powers of enforcement. This means that consumers have to take the company to court in a civil action, rather than officers taking the case to court on behalf of the public. Winning a civil action would probably lead to the consumer receiving some money back. A public prosecution would probably have led to a fine and the company would have to show that it took reasonable precautions in making its original claims.

The directive will also require travel companies to lodge a **bond,** sufficient to cover themselves if they cease trading. Trading standards officers will have the task of assessing what the level of cover should be for each company. Given the size and complicated structure of the largest tour operators, this may prove to be a very difficult task.

## Your tasks

1 Identify a specific package tour offer, advertised in a holiday brochure. Note all the claims made about the destination, the accommodation, the travel arrangements, the facilities and services offered and the price.

2 Discuss the claims and then decide, in the event of a dispute between customer and company, under which of the two following headings you would list them:
   **a)** those which would be easy to verify
   **b)** those which would be hard to prove.

3 Read all the small print in the brochure. Identify all the areas where the company disclaims liability for things which might happen before or on the holiday.

4 Discuss each of these conditions and agree under which of the following two headings you would list them:
   **a)** those which are reasonable precautions for any company to take
   **b)** those which some customers might argue were an attempt to take advantage of them.

5 Write an advertisement for a planned school journey or holiday which you think would give you adequate protection against prosecution.

# Glossary

**base rate**  the rate which banks use to determine the interest they will charge to borrowers

**bequests**  sums of money or property left in a will to another person or organisation

**bond**  a sum of money held on behalf of a company, to be used to refund their customers should the company go out of business

**capital works**  major fixed investment usually associated with buildings or equipment and often funded by long term loans or directly out of company profits

**cash flow**  the movement of money received and paid out by a business

**charitable trust**  a non-profit-making organisation overseeing the use of funds often donated specifically for the upkeep and management of property or estates

**contingency plan**  a plan made in order to be ready for the occurrence of some chance or unexpected situation

**crime audit**  a detailed assessment of the crime risks in a specific location and the remedial actions which these might require

**deeds of covenant**  legal agreements usually covering a set period and often involving the contribution of funds to another person or organisation

**directives**  decisions passed on as instructions from one organisation having authority over others

**documentation**  all the written paperwork which supports a business transaction

**endowment**  money which is settled on a specific property in order to maintain and restore it

**English Tourist Board**  a national government-funded organisation aiming to encourage the British to take more holidays in England and to improve the facilities available to them when they do

**ethos**  the type of behaviour and atmosphere which is characteristic of an organisation

**freehold**  property which the owner is free to dispose of or pass on as an inheritance

**legacy**  money or personal property left in a will

**liability**  responsibility to protect clients against risk

**market value**  the current price which potential purchasers are willing to pay for goods or services

**media**  means by which information is passed on to the public, for example newspapers, radio, television

**networked**  linked into a system of computer terminals which can pass information to one another

**premium payment**  a single sum of money paid for insurance

**private sector**  businesses owned and operated by private individuals and firms

**privatise**  to convert a business or organisation from government funding to private ownership

**pro forma**  a document or form in which the layout and wording has been standardised

**public sector**  organisations and businesses financed by government funds

**regeneration**  the rebuilding and revitalising of areas such as city centres

**remortgage**  borrowing an additional sum of money using the increased value of property as security

**retail travel**  the process of selling travel arrangements directly to customers

**security**  land or property offered as a guarantee against the repayment of a loan

**source markets**  the area from which potential customers are derived

**subsidiary**  a less important branch of a company, but one which contributes to their overall profit

**tagging**  a system of using labels attached to goods which set off an alarm if they are removed from the premises

**target markets**  the consumer groups to which a company is aiming to sell its products and services

**Tourist Information Centre**  a centre providing information about transport, accommodation and attractions in the surrounding area

**turnover**  the money value of a company's total sales and other income over a specified period

**viability**  the likelihood of a business or scheme being successful